DIVORCE RECOVERY FOR TEENAGERS

Zondervan/Youth Specialties Books

Adventure Games
Amazing Tension Getters
Called to Care
The Complete Student Missions Handbook
Creative Socials and Special Events
Divorce Recovery for Teenagers
Feeding Your Forgotten Soul (Spiritual Growth for Youth Workers)
Get 'Em Talking
Good Clean Fun
Good Clean Fun, Volume 2
Great Games for 4th-6th Graders (Get 'Em Growing)
Great Ideas for Small Youth Groups
Greatest Skits on Earth
Greatest Skits on Earth, Volume 2
Growing Up in America
High School Ministry
High School TalkSheets
Holiday Ideas for Youth Groups (Revised Edition)
Hot Talks
Ideas for Social Action
Intensive Care: Helping Teenagers in Crisis
Junior High Ministry
Junior High TalkSheets
The Ministry of Nurture
On-Site: 40 On-Location Programs for Youth Groups
Option Plays
Organizing Your Youth Ministry
Play It! Great Games for Groups
Teaching the Bible Creatively
Teaching the Truth about Sex
Tension Getters
Tension Getters II
Unsung Heroes: How to Recruit and Train Volunteer Youth Workers
Up Close and Personal: How to Build Community in Your Youth Group
Youth Specialties Clip Art Book
Youth Specialties Clip Art Book, Volume 2

DIVORCE RECOVERY FOR TEENAGERS

STEPHEN MURRAY
AND RANDY SMITH

ZondervanPublishingHouse

Grand Rapids, Michigan

A Division of HarperCollinsPublishers

All case histories are composites, and the names of people used in the stories are fictitious.

Divorce Recovery for Teenagers

Copyright © 1990 by Youth Specialties, Inc.

Youth Specialties Books, 1224 Greenfield Drive, El Cajon, California 92021,
are published by Zondervan Publishing House,
1415 Lake Drive, S.E., Grand Rapids, Michigan 49506

Library of Congress Cataloging-in-Publication Data

Murray, Stephen, 1954-
    Divorce recovery for teenagers: how to help your kids recover, heal, and grow when their families are
    ripped apart/by Stephen Murray and Randy Smith.
        p.   cm.
    ISBN 0-310-53151-9
    1. Church work with teenagers. 2. Children of divorced parents—Religious life. 3. Children of divorced
    parents—Pastoral counseling of. I. Smith, Randy, 1951– . II. Title.
    BV4447.M82 1990
    259'.23—dc20   90-33479
                                                                                                                          CIP

Edited by J. Cheri McLaughlin
Designed by Michael Kern

Printed in the United States of America

90 91 92 93 94 95 96 97 98 99 /   / 10 9 8 7 6 5 4 3 2 1

About the YouthSource™ Publishing Group

YouthSource™ books, tapes, videos, and other resources pool the expertise of three of the finest youth-ministry resource providers in the world:

- **Campus Life Books**—publishers of the award-winning *Campus Life* magazine, who for nearly fifty years have helped high schoolers live Christian lives.

- **Youth Specialties**—serving ministers to middle-school, junior-high, and high-school youth for over twenty years through books, magazines, and training events such as the National Youth Workers Convention.

- **Zondervan Publishing House**—one of the oldest, largest, and most respected evangelical Christian publishers in the world.

Campus Life	**Youth Specialties**	**Zondervan**
465 Gundersen Dr.	1224 Greenfield Dr.	1415 Lake Dr. S.E.
Carol Stream, IL 60188	El Cajon, CA 92021	Grand Rapids, MI 49506
708/260-6200	619/440-2333	616/698-6900

To the students, adult volunteers, and ministry colleagues who helped us learn about divorce-recovery ministry and develop the format and content for the Adolescent Divorce Recovery Workshop.

CONTENTS

FOREWORD

Divorce Recovery for Teenagers is, in my estimation, one of the most valuable resources for directing ministry to teenagers whose families are experiencing the anguish of divorce. Instead of engaging in "the paralysis of analysis," Stephen Murray and Randy Smith go beyond theory to provide pastors and Christian leaders with a how-to manual for hands-on ministry to adolescents in a divorce recovery workshop.

For the last eight years I have watched hundreds of reluctant kids dragged to this workshop, kids who have been bribed and coerced to come by their parents. What a joy it has been to be a part of their experience on the final night, hearing so many of them express regret and sorrow that the workshop is ending. They want more! Many of them have come back again, either to retake the workshop or to serve as discussion leaders.

This book has been born out of the experience, creativity, trial and error, and teamwork practiced during many of these workshops. The workshops explained in *Divorce Recovery for Teenagers* are comprehensive programs that help teenagers to deal with the pain of divorced parents and to experience healing and wholeness by coming to grips with their feelings and hurts. Kids come away from the workshop with principles that bring stability and wholeness to their lives once more.

Stephen and Randy have prepared an excellent resource for anyone who shares with them the burden of bringing healing to a particular and very widespread hurt within the body of Christ. My sincere prayer is that you will use the message of health and hope in this book to touch many young lives with wholeness and with the love of Christ.

Bill Flanagan
Newport Beach, California
February, 1990

ACKNOWLEDGMENTS

Special thanks to St. Andrew's Presbyterian Church and Youth Specialties for ongoing support and guidance throughout this project. And thanks to our families, for they are the reason we are committed to helping young people experience the best they can in their own families, both now and in the future.

Stephen Murray
Randy Smith

INTRODUCTION

"I still remember the day when my parents sat me and my brother down to tell us they were getting divorced. I had a sick feeling in the pit of my stomach. My worst nightmare was coming true, just like it had for so many of my friends. I was now going to be a kid from a broken home! Actually it wasn't as bad as I thought it would be. But even after five years, I still feel really sad sometimes. Will I ever get over it?"

"It's really weird now that my mom is dating again. The thought of some other guy trying to be my dad is too weird for me. Especially since the guy is such a geek. My real dad is living with a woman only eight years older than me—and he wants me to be friends with her! She broke up my parents' marriage! What should I do?"

"I'm seventeen, but I'm too distrustful of guys to enjoy dating—I was dumped by my last boyfriend. Boys are so immature! Is there something wrong with me, or what? What if I end up getting a divorce someday like my parents did?"

"Since I became a Christian last summer, I feel more guilty than ever when my mom wants me to spend time with her and I don't. She says I have an attitude problem, but it's her fault she's alone. It's almost like she wants me to be the dad. Plus, she resents it when I spend time with my dad at his place, and she always gives me the third degree when I come home! How do I tell her that I have my own life to live? I love her, but this seems so unfair."

What would you tell these teenagers? What do you tell those kids in your youth group who have the same questions? And what about the kids who aren't willing to even ask the question or who aren't even aware that there are questions to be asked or answers to be found?

Divorce is not an unforgivable sin that creates broken families. Divorce changes families, divorce wounds families, but to say that divorce "breaks" families is to rob them of their ability to recover. And recover they must, if the children are to learn better ways of choosing marriage partners and staying married.

In the spring of 1981, Dr. Bill Flanagan began an adult divorce recovery workshop through St. Andrew's Presbyterian Church in Newport Beach, California. The following fall, at Dr. Flanagan's suggestion, we began discussing the possibility of establishing a similar workshop for the teenage children of the adult workshop participants.

The need for the teenage workshop, which first began in spring of 1982, proved overwhelming. We have to offer two workshops per year—one in the fall and one in the spring. To date, over seventeen workshops averaging forty adolescent participants each have seen success similar to the adult workshops, which have been attended by over four thousand participants.

We have written *Divorce Recovery for Teenagers* in response to many questions that youth workers across the country have asked about our workshop format and techniques. It provides basic theology and a practical curriculum for youth workers coping with the realities of divorce in their own church communities.

While there are many books about divorce recovery available to adults and an increasing number of books available to teenagers, there is next to nothing for the potential workshop leader. *Divorce Recovery for Teenagers* is not a study of the effects of divorce on teenagers, nor is it a manual on counseling techniques (although we do discuss helpful strategies in working with teenagers). It is an attempt to communicate to fellow youth workers that divorce recovery for teens is not only possible but necessary. We share practical suggestions from our experiences in grappling with the difficult issues created by divorce. We hope to orient, prepare, alert, and above all encourage you by identifying key concepts that have led teens through divorce recovery.

We don't expect everyone to agree with everything we say. Many churches, for example, are reluctant to conduct divorce recovery workshops for fear they will appear to be advocating divorce. We are not pro divorce. We are pro family. Those who have ministered with split families know that negative factors leading into and arising from divorce don't magically resolve themselves when the divorce becomes final. Since the divorce-recovery process needs to include caring people outside the immediate family, our ministry staff has risked doing workshops in an effort to be salt and light in the world.

We invite you to join us in helping young people who want to heal from the painful effects of divorce. There is in such ministry the opportunity to spread knowledge of the wonderful hope that Jesus Christ offers these teenagers and their families. By the grace of God, may we all be counted among those who share that hope.

Stephen Murray and Randy Smith
Newport Beach, California

SECTION ONE

THE IMPACT OF DIVORCE ON TEENAGERS

1
MINISTERING TO FAMILIES IN DIVORCE

Stephen Murray

Regardless of how you view divorce, your church and community have adolescents who hurt from it. This book assumes you've already discovered at least one of these hurting teens whose parents' divorce is either underway or an accomplished fact. Or perhaps you know of teens who live in a single-parent home or are part of a blended family or whose parent has a live-in boyfriend or girlfriend. Whether these teens show outward signs of distress directly related to divorce or not, you may be wondering how you might more effectively minister to them.

Before you start guiding a teen through divorce recovery, you must think through your personal theology of divorce and recovery. Before you begin helping teens to cope with life in a single-parent home or a blended family, you need to identify the issues teens face in those situations. Before you attempt to be part of their healing process, you need to understand the attitudes and skills required of a healer.

We are not attempting to provide a fully developed theology of divorce, since such a treatment would require a separate book. Simply stated, however, our premise for understanding divorce is that God's law is fulfilled by God's grace; and God's grace is available to all people. We guide our teaching and counseling by a three-point theology of divorce:

- Divorce is always a tragic event that goes against God's will for his people.
- In a sinful world divorce is sometimes inevitable and even necessary.
- Our response to those who divorce needs to emphasize mourning, acceptance, forgiveness, grace, truth, repentance, and hope.

Let's look briefly at these three assertions.

- **Divorce is always a tragic event that goes against God's will for his people.**

As an associate pastor in a church of over 3,500 members, I conduct many weddings each year. Our wedding policy requires all couples to attend two premarital seminars, take the Taylor-Johnson Temperament Analysis, and spend several counseling sessions with the pastor prior to the ceremony. We do everything we can to help couples prepare for marriage. A wedding doesn't make a marriage work—a wedding is simply a beautiful way to begin a marriage.

Marriage is ordained by God for the benefit and happiness of humankind. Wedding vows express the responsibilities of a man and woman who desire to enjoy that happiness and those benefits. A committed man, a committed woman, and a committed Lord make a marriage work. Nowhere in the wedding vows is there a clause that allows for divorce. Nowhere in Scripture is divorce treated as part of God's plan for marriage. Jesus said that Moses wrote in the clause on divorce because of human weakness, disobedience, and rebellion (Mark 10:5). Divorce is always an offense to God and a sign of failure.

Everyone loses in divorce: the couple, their kids, their family, their friends—even society. The gains derived from a divorce don't compensate for the greater loss of God's ideal—which is one man married to one woman until death parts them. Divorce is a last-ditch resort after all attempts at restoration and reconciliation have failed.

In our church we therefore approach divorce-recovery ministry with a deep sense of pain for what a family in divorce is experiencing and has experienced, but we do not stand in judgment over anyone. While divorce is an obvious sin, we all have sins that, though perhaps less obvious, are nonetheless also sins. As Jesus pointed out to those who were eager to stone the adulteress, none of us are without sin (John 8:7).

Our goal in the divorce-recovery process is to help kids who, though not responsible for the divorce, must learn to live with its consequences. We are simply trying to salvage what we can for the rebuilding process ahead. While we talk with teens about losses and gains because of divorce, we don't imply that there is anything to be gained from a divorce that couldn't have been achieved within the marriage (peace and quiet, for example). We don't treat divorce lightly. Neither do we approach those in divorcing families with harsh judgment. It is because divorce is such a serious matter that we emphasize responding with forgiveness and grace. Before we discuss this theological aspect, let's consider the realities of divorce.

• In a sinful world divorce is sometimes inevitable and even necessary.

Although we don't advocate divorce, we recognize it exists. It's a reality that confronts us daily. Do we err in making the bold assertion that divorce is sometimes inevitable and even necessary? If so, we choose to err on the side of fact; because of human frailty, weakness, and evil, divorce happens.

In what sense is divorce sometimes inevitable? When one partner abandons the marriage and files for divorce, for instance, divorce is usually inevitable. In what sense is divorce necessary? Physical and psychological abuse or extramarital affairs often push people to consider divorce as a means of protecting one's self and one's children from the effects of a self-destructive spouse.

Although the Scriptures never sanction divorce, divorce is grudgingly allowed. Jesus, in Matthew 19:3–12, explains that Moses allowed divorce because of the hardness of our hearts. He goes on to say that divorce is allowed in the case of marital unfaithfulness. But what is marital unfaithfulness? Given the vagueness of the Greek word *porneia*, from which this phrase is translated, marital unfaithfulness is anything that demeans the marriage vows. The rabbis of Jesus' time debated this thoroughly, and one prominent school of thought allowed a divorce certificate to be given for the most trivial reasons.

At what point is a person so injured by marital unfaithfulness that a divorce is the only solution to the marital trauma? Only the partner who chooses to divorce knows the subjective answer to that question. Jesus doesn't say that one *must* divorce because of marital unfaithfulness. He merely says that divorce is *permitted* under such circumstances.

Certainly, then, the first job of the Christian minister and counselor is to work with the couple toward reconciliation—if the couple is willing. Unfortunately, a family often comes for help only after the decision to divorce has been made and acted upon. How do we respond to the divorced in our midst? In particular, how do we help their children deal effectively with divorce?

• Our response to those who divorce needs to emphasize mourning, acceptance, forgiveness, grace, truth, repentance, and hope.

From the fullness of his grace, in fulfillment of the Law, Jesus ministers grace to us. His life and teachings offer us four pictures of restoration: the parable of the good Samaritan (Luke 10:25–37), the parable of the prodigal son (Luke 15:11–32), his conversation with the woman at the well (John 4:1–26), and his encounter with the woman caught in adultery (John 8:3–11).

Our response to divorced families takes its cue from these lessons, for in each case Jesus confronts evil and is full of grace and truth without violating the Law. Each encounter portrays a godly person's dismay with sin, a self-righteous person's spiritual pride, and a fallen person's need for grace. In fact, mourning, acceptance, forgiveness, grace, truth, repentance, and hope are the support pillars of effective ministry among divorced parents and their children.

Mourning. We mourn the loss of God's ideal for marital benefits and happiness in a family. We mourn that the children of this family won't have both natural parents at home to create an environment of stability, love, discipline, guidance, and material provision. We mourn that a couple who started out with dreams of marital fulfillment and family harmony now find themselves sharing custody of their kids or perhaps losing regular access to their children. We mourn that, in the midst of adolescent instability, a young person faces the turmoil of divorce.

When a parent dies, children experience a sense of finality born of circumstance. When a couple divorces, kids more often feel betrayed and rejected because their parents *chose* to split the family. Feelings of being betrayed or rejected create a troubling reality for adolescents. When a marriage dies, a dream also dies—a dream for a happy marriage, a dream for a happy family life, and a dream for two parents who love each other to share that love together with their children. Our dreams, as opposed to our fantasies, represent our hopes in all of life's possibilities. When dreams die we grieve their loss.

You can express your grief over the pain of a young person by saying something like, "It breaks my heart that you went through the pain of your parents' divorce." If a teen is vulnerable to the point of tears, you might just cry together. Often, however, a teen won't admit he's hurting. Or he if he's experiencing emotional turmoil, he may not connect his pain with his parents' divorce. Letting a kid hear or see your mourning on his behalf can free him to acknowledge and confront his own pain.

Teens express their grief in statements like, "I never thought this would happen to me," "I guess life is just that way," or "Why did this have to happen?" In cases where they won't even talk about it, they adapt to the new circumstances by ignoring their losses and inadvertently consigning their grief to a growing reservoir of pain deep within themselves.

It's not unusual for kids to have no felt need to talk about their parents' divorce because they've decided to mourn in silence, or not to mourn at all. If they were very young when the divorce occurred, their conscious memory may not include the death of a dream. As they grow up they will learn what they lost, however, and mourning allows them to name and feel their grief—and in naming it rob it of its power to destroy. It allows a person to begin the process of building a future on top of the ashes of the past. Mourning brings closure to one chapter of life, providing a bookmark for the rest of the story.

Acceptance. Although the waiting father in the parable of the prodigal didn't approve of his wayward son's behavior, he treated him with respect and unconditional love. That's what we mean when we talk about accepting people where they are. Acceptance, however, is not indulgence. The prodigal's father allowed his son to face the consequences of his errant behavior. He did not rescue his son, but let him eat with the pigs until the boy hated it. When the boy decided to leave the pigs behind, the father was already waiting to receive him back.

Indulgent love, on the other hand, fosters co-dependent or enabling behavior. In essence it means that we become part of the problem rather than part of the solution. While unconditional love allows for change, indulgent love inhibits it. Unconditional love fosters healthy independence, whereas indulgent love creates an unhealthy dependency. Unconditional acceptance of others grants them the dignity they need to claim their birthright as children of God; indulgent love makes them a prisoner.

Offering acceptance is not the same as granting permission or approval. Our ability to accept others shows how much we are willing and able to deal with reality. To accept a person or a situation is to say, "Hey, this is what is." Withholding acceptance is a misguided effort at avoiding a compromise of truth. Withholding acceptance is instead clinging to what we wish a person or situation would be like. Acceptance requires us to be active. In place of passively saying, "Oh well," we actively seek God's leading. "How can I be your witness in this situation?" is our prayer. Such an attitude compels us to confront a fallen world with God's love and justice. It seeks the lost sheep until they are found.

Thus, when the church accepts the wounded, it becomes God's hands and voice, transforming people and situations. The gospel triumphs and the kingdom of God advances. When the church refuses to accept people as they are, then the church forfeits its role as the light of the world (Matt. 5:14). The light is placed under a bushel. God is rendered silent if we step around the broken body in the path before us, leaving it to the compassion of the Samaritan. The good Samaritans outside the church are willing to accept people and help them, *but they are not able to teach words of eternal life.* Yet until we accept others, neither are we able.

We need to accept especially the children of divorce, modeling for them accepting their parents and accepting the reality of their situation. We dare not take sides or paper over the circumstances that led to a divorce. I personally have a hard time with this because I often see how parents' selfishness hurts their children. I need to accept parents who have sinned as wounded people as well. Only my own arrogance makes it difficult for me to accept others.

An effective recovery ministry grows out of *unconditional* acceptance of the participants. Such acceptance is given in a fashion accountable to the doctrines and disciplines of your church and in the context of Jesus' mandate to love others as he loved us. Practically speaking, your acceptance of others is measured by your willingness to take action in a messy situation. Acceptance does not mean compromising your beliefs or values. You simply make yourself available to God so that he might use you in the lives of those who are ready to receive help—those who are sick of eating with the pigs. Like the gift of the father to his prodigal son, your acceptance of families in turmoil offers them the possibility of a fresh start.

Forgiveness. People in need of forgiveness are also in need of second chances. This includes a second chance at marriage. Some people may be unfit to remarry, but most divorced people will eventually desire to remarry. If a church hangs in there with divorced families, it can help subsequent marriages be strong. If it refuses to forgive and support these new families, its rejection can help set them up for repeated failures.

Forgiveness is probably one of the most difficult things we are commanded to do by the Lord. It usually requires time for the healing of hurts. If Christians demonstrate a forgiving attitude toward divorced families, they practice the biblical injunction to forgive one another (Eph. 4:32). Those of us who work with families in divorce cannot mandate forgiveness between parents and children, but we can nurture their capacity to forgive as we work alongside of them on rebuilding their lives.

Forgiveness is about letting go of the hate and hurt that tenaciously cling within all of our hearts at times. The focus should be on *my* problem with *my* feelings, not on someone else's offense, perceived or real. Those who forgive are able to get on with their lives rather

I COULDN'T FORGIVE HIM

My parents divorced when I was four years old, and I have always lived with my mom and my younger brother and sister. As long as I can remember, my dad has been the kind of person who makes promises that he doesn't keep. Like the times when it was his weekend to have us kids over and he would promise to pick us up on Friday after school. Many times we waited around for several hours before he showed up. Sometimes he never even came—he would finally call to say he wasn't coming because he had to work late. I always felt so hurt and angry, and I would call him up and yell at him. He would apologize and promise not to do it again. But he did.

I would ask him to come to swim meets or track meets or school plays, and he would always promise to be there, only to disappoint me by not showing up. He made excuses, apologized, and promised to make it up to me. I wanted to believe it, so I made myself get over my hurt feelings and anger. Every time I let my hopes get up again, the same thing would always happen. Each time he broke a promise, all my hurt feelings and anger from the past would well up in me and overwhelm me. It was like I was handling my anger toward my dad as I would handle a kite. I would put my hurt and anger (the kite) out of mind, but never really let go of it (I still held the string).

I am now in my senior year of high school, and I really thought that everything was great with me and my dad. I even went with him to the homecoming reunion at his college, which is nearby, and I had a really fun weekend. But when I recently turned eighteen, he stopped sending my mom child support for me, since he was no longer obligated by law to pay it. He knows that my mom is working two jobs to support me and my sister and brother and that we all have part-time jobs in order to help pay the bills each month. We live a simple life and can afford no luxuries. Meanwhile, he is living very comfortably.

When my mom broke the news to me, I was stunned because he had told me that he would continue to pay the child support and also that he would pay for my college tuition. Maybe this meant that he wasn't going to help me go to college. All the old feelings came back, and I vowed never to talk to him again until he changed.

But then I realized that he'll probably never change, and I can never change him. He is not able or willing to make or keep commitments. I suppose that's why he and my mom got divorced and why his second wife also left him. I finally accepted that and was able to let go of the string. Sometimes the old feelings come back, but now I just let them go when they do. I accept my dad the way he is and keep my expectations of him in check.

It's funny, 'cause now I also feel more free to accept other people with all their weaknesses. My dad makes a lot of promises that he can't keep because he wants to look good in my eyes. And he buries himself in guilt when he fails. Understanding him has helped me to forgive the past, even if I can't totally forget it. It has also helped me to keep short accounts in the present. I don't completely understand why forgiveness works, I just know it does.

than be stuck in a cycle of negative emotions. Gina would repeatedly forgive her father, but only to be manipulated again by his empty promises of change. She would then reclaim all the negative feelings from the past and up the ante of her hate for him. She realized that she was not truly forgiving her father but rather was making an exchange with him: "If you change and mean it, then I will forgive you; but if you disappoint me, then you are no longer forgiven."

Gina learned to let go of the past at the point when she could unilaterally forgive her father. Now she is learning to understand what makes her dad tick, and she is able to deal with him based on the present rather than solely on his past performances. After letting go of any debts her father may have owed her, she is free to take their relationship as it is rather than as she had always hoped it would be. Through the workshop Gina learned to take charge of her life by accepting responsibility for her feelings. She learned how to give forgiveness to and receive forgiveness from others.

Grace. It is through a generous application of God's grace that we forgive and restore people from divorced families. This grace fulfills the requirements of the Law, because Jesus' death covers our sin. It is by the authority of Jesus—not by our own righteousness—that we can receive and minister God's grace. The Atonement affects every human relationship, including divorce. Teens need to hear that God's grace will enable them to overcome the adverse effects of divorce and to grow into whole people.

Grace provides the fuel for the church to become part of God's reconciliating work in the world. Obviously we need to avoid cheapening the grace of God by carefully instructing and counseling those who come to us to be married or remarried. Will some abuse this grace? Most certainly. At that point, we who minister must exercise tough love and direct people to that which is true, right, and good. For some couples that means we will not

marry them—not because we judge them, but to fulfill our role of pastoring them, getting close to them. Tough love means asking a couple who wants to remarry, "Do you really understand what this first marriage failure meant? Have you dealt with the problems that broke up your first marriage?"

Thus we let families in divorce know that it is never too late to turn their lives around. It is never too late to repent. The power for change is found in the grace God lavishly showers on us. It's always there, even when we're oblivious to it. Grace never wanes, never runs low.

When it comes to ministering God's grace, I find that I am often in the same situation as the main character (played by Raymond Burr) in the television program of the early sixties called *The Millionaire.* His job was to deliver a check for one million dollars to some fortunate individual selected by an anonymous millionaire. The whole show was about Burr trying to convince these lucky people that the check was good, that it was theirs to spend—no strings attached. All they had to do was accept it and enjoy it.

That is an accurate analogy for those who minister the expanse of God's grace to those convinced that it is too good to be true. The people in *The Millionaire* inevitably became convinced that Raymond Burr—the bearer of the gift—had brought them a genuine check. They quickly changed from cynical skeptics into deliriously happy millionaires.

As we bring the Good News of God's grace to those we work with, they must experience something of it in us in order to believe it exists. The Holy Spirit works to convince these people that "salvation has come to this house" (Luke 19:9) and that they can receive God's riches at Christ's expense. Often their belief in God is quickened as they perceive us to be accepting, forgiving, gracious, truthful, and hopeful.

Truth. We who facilitate divorce recovery need to speak the truth plainly and with love. We dare not tell people what they want to hear. The truth we proclaim is that divorce has serious consequences, that it is akin to amputating a limb in order to save a life. Divorce in itself doesn't solve anything. It requires a process of recovery whereby a family recognizes what went wrong, takes responsibility for it, and moves ahead. Young people need to be assured that they can grow through divorce and not be doomed to repeat their parents' marital mistakes. They must be confronted with the privileges and the responsibilities of marriage, and they must be challenged to learn from their parents' divorce.

The workshop format is a learning process whereby participants gain insight into understanding and coping with reality. Hopefully, they will also learn to create a reality they can enjoy. To create that kind of reality, kids must stop telling themselves, "I'm stuck in this lousy situation." You can help them stop by responding, "Let's talk about being stuck. What would you like to see happen?"

If a young person is open to talk at that point, he might say something like, "I don't like it when my mom brings a guy home to spend the night. I feel like there's nothing I can do about it." One kid I know took the car out and cruised all night whenever his mom went out on a date. The kid was twelve years old. His mom asked Randy what she should do. Randy said, "Call the police."

At first it seemed like too drastic a measure, but she followed through on her next date. Her son got arrested and that got his attention. He and his mom agreed they needed counseling, and they were able to get beyond the behavior of illegal driving to the real issue—his feelings about his mom dating. They both learned that they liked it better when they talked things out instead of acting out.

Warn kids not to believe the lie that things are hopeless. Tell them not to wait for someone else to make them happy. Life is more than emotions. It is volition as well. A young person can choose to be different, to relate more maturely. If truth is a map of reality, then we want to help young people and their families correct their inaccurate maps. We do this by teaching and discussing the skills essential to recovery and growth—skills like negotiation, acknowledging gains, being responsible for me, and reaching out to God.

Repentance. Those who are recovering from divorce need to hear about repentance in such a way that they can understand it as an act of will that allows us to receive the grace of God. Adults and teens alike generally dismiss the word *repent* as a guilt-inducing holdover from itinerant evangelists on the sawdust trail. The process of repentance, however, is a series of decisions to choose life over death and hope over despair.

Change or repentance is an act of will. Yet repentance is also the process by which we become willing to change. Repentance includes many points of turning, and those who would repent must put their destructive, self-defeating behavior (sin) behind them. Repentance involves a new start, followed by the process of growing in a new direction. In our workshops we challenge people to turn in a new direction, take charge of their lives, and grow in wholeness. We urge people to become born again by showing them the necessary steps to take toward recovery and by showing them how they need God to endure through the process of recovery.

We respect the recovery aspect of the workshop format by not being blatantly evangelistic, so non-Christians can feel comfortable attending and gain a measure of recovery. We don't think of the divorce recovery workshop as a way to fake people into coming to hear the gospel. But we do make it clear that Jesus Christ has done what it takes to give us all the chance to make a fresh start. Hosting the workshop in a Christian church reinforces any evangelistic message we give. Is anyone ever saved through the workshop? Sometimes. But more often people are saved as the result of Christians coming alongside them in times of crisis and pain. I view the workshop in the same way that I view the stretcher on which the paralytic was lowered through the roof by his friends. It is a means to position people so that they can encounter the healing love of Jesus.

Hope. You can convey an attitude of hopefulness to young people by instructing them in the psychological, emotional, and spiritual factors of continued growth and development. You give them hope as you teach coping techniques, give them insight into human behavior, and help them sharpen their spiritual awareness. You reinforce your lessons by showing warm acceptance of them—just as they are.

People need hope to rally their energies, and energy is necessary for them to grow through the inevitable challenges of life. By conveying hope you help young people who feel like victims to develop a sense of personal power. They learn to use this power creatively at home and beyond.

The Apostle Paul says that our hope is found in God's grace, which is made available to us in the midst of our suffering at exactly the right time (Rom. 5:1–8). "At a time like this I need the Lord to help me," is how an old song goes. That's certainly true in the case of divorce. When there seems to be little if any hope for new dreams, God's love meets us at the point of our powerlessness and reconstructs our vision for new hope.

Although psychologically hope initially feels the same to those who receive it, we who minister hope know that only in the context of eternal hope does earthly hope finds its fulfillment. Unbelievers can experience aspects of hope, but the fullness of hope can only come from God through Jesus Christ. We hold up hope as the reward for those who embrace and grow through their sufferings.

Greg shuffled into one of our workshops thinking that his whole life was ruined by his parents' divorce. He had settled into a grim acceptance that nothing would ever get better. After that workshop he wanted to come back as a student leader. He told me, "I feel like I'm seeing my problems through different eyes. I really feel like things might change for the better soon." The workshop had validated his feelings and equipped him to choose to act differently in response to those emotions.

His dad later attended the adult workshop, and Greg saw big changes afterward. Greg received Christ shortly after attending the workshop and has gone on to be an effective worker for Campus Crusade. Recalling his first workshop he later wrote me, "The workshop helped me understand what I was feeling and why. It also showed me that I was not alone in my situation. Most importantly, it gave me hope."

In Summary

While we do everything we can to help couples prepare for marriage, only a committed man, a committed woman, and a committed Lord make a marriage work. The Scriptures allow divorce because of human weakness, disobedience, and rebellion, but divorce is always an offense to God and a sign of failure. Everyone loses in divorce. Although we do not advocate divorce, we recognize it exists. And while we desire reconciliation, a family often comes for help only after the decision to divorce has been made and acted upon. So our response to the divorced family must emphasize mourning, acceptance, forgiveness, grace, truth, repentance, and hope. ♥

2
WHAT TEENAGERS GO THROUGH WHEN THEIR PARENTS DIVORCE

Randy Smith

Divorce is a crisis event for children of all ages. Divorce is usually preceded by painful and disturbing experiences in the family. When we began ministering to kids of divorcing families, we learned to expect an emotionally intense and challenging experience.

When you begin to deal with kids of divorce, you come face to face with sin and sickness in our society—selfishness, affairs, violence, alcohol and drug abuse, and more. You also encounter the intense emotions of pain, anger, and fear that go with these problems.

NO SURPRISE   Stacey's Story

I'm fifteen years old, and to anybody looking at me and my family from the outside, it looks like we've got it all together. Dad makes good money so we live in a "good" neighborhood, and I'm in the honors classes at my high school. We go to church every Sunday, and I'm even a leader in the youth group. Dad coaches my little brother's Boys Club basketball team. But looks aren't everything.

I don't invite my friends over to spend the night any more because Mom and Dad yell at each other—even in front of company. I don't remember them ever being happy together. They're either fighting about the way Mom spends money, or Mom is giving Dad the silent treatment because of their last fight. Dad always picks on the littlest things about both me and Mom. Nothing is ever good enough for him. I got all A's last semester, except

for a B in biology. All he talked about was that B. That's what happens when you talk on the phone instead of doing your homework, was his final remark.

Last week I overheard Mom talking to her sister. I guess she's heard from someone at Dad's work that his recent "business trips" had nothing to do with business. I didn't want to hear any more. But I had to listen to it when they started fighting that night. Dad said he was moving out to live with another woman. At first I wanted to crash into their room and yell at Dad. I wanted to tell him what a selfish brat he was being. What about us kids? But instead I just put a pillow over my head and cried.

Now that I've thought about it more, maybe it's for the best. I could use a break from his criticism, and it'll be a relief to go to bed at night and be able to fall asleep in peace and quiet. But still, he's my dad.

My folks owned a quick-print business. Me and my older brother worked there after school. My little sister just sort of hung out. She helped stock shelves for Mom sometimes. Mom and Dad have always worked hard, and so have us kids. But every year we've taken a family vacation together. Last year we spent a whole week at Disney World.

That's why I was so amazed when Mom and Dad sat me down and told me that Dad was moving out of the house and selling Mom his part of the business. I mean, sure there's been tension sometimes between them. But I figured it was the pressure of the business or something.

They told me I was going to stay with Mom—they didn't give me any choice in the matter or even ask what I thought about their divorce. But then I was so shocked that I couldn't think of anything intelligent to say anyway.

They never talked about the divorce again. It just happened.

That was two years ago. After the divorce Dad went to work for one of our biggest clients setting up their own print shop. He married the lady that used to handle all their print jobs. Mom still runs our business, but she complains about Dad's workaholism and says his new marriage won't last either. I just try to keep busy.

Bill's story could not be more different than Stacey's. After years of listening to teens tell their stories, we learned that divorce experiences are as diverse as families, ranging from quiet to raging, from proximate to scattered throughout the country, from reasonably calm to painfully violent. To get a balanced perspective on the teen's experience of divorce and to help us remember that divorce is merely one part of an ongoing process, we talk about divorce as an experience of pain, of gain, and of change.

Dealing with Pain in Divorce

No matter what the details of the story, we have noticed that to one degree or another kids are hurt and disillusioned by divorce. Divorce brings pain. And the pain of divorce takes many forms. Most children, whether perceived to be handling a divorce well or not, feel abandoned, neglected, abused, and smothered when their parents divorce. They are also left with a dysfunctional model of marriage that can set them up for marital failure themselves.

Abandonment

When a significant person in a teen's life just leaves, that teen experiences an intense feeling of loss. Commonly a child's father moves away after the divorce and rarely visits his kids. Perhaps his employer transfers him, or maybe his new wife wishes to live elsewhere. Sometimes a man tries to escape feelings of pain or guilt by putting physical distance between himself and his kids and ex-wife. The cause is not as important to kids as the fact that they feel they have been abandoned.

Neglect

Another experience common to children of divorce, neglect happens when parents are so caught up in their conflict that they don't pay enough attention to kids' developmental needs for affirmation, nurturing, correction, and guidance. Parents sometimes neglect even their children's fundamental needs for food, clothing, shelter, and medical attention.

The process of a marriage breaking down and the subsequent divorce drains energy from the adults, energy that is normally expended in parenting. Parents obsessed and worn down by their conflict are emotionally unavailable for the kids. Even if they are handling it well emotionally, a parent who manages a single-parent home and works full-time has less energy for

My two younger brothers and I had been to two divorce recovery workshops. I could see how I had experienced some of the different stages of grieving over my dad leaving us. At first I didn't want to believe Dad was divorcing Mom to marry a stewardess on the airline he used for business trips. Then I got just plain mad at him—and her, too.

I told Dad I would miss him if he left us, but I guess my feelings weren't as important to him as I thought. When he tried to explain everything, I just felt really tired, and I didn't want to look at him. For a while I felt ashamed of Mom and Dad, and I felt like everybody knew what was happening in our family, so I stayed in my room a lot. But my friends were great. They started to call me, and when they found out Dad had left, a couple of them told me their Dads had done the same thing, and they had lived through it. So would I, they said.

My brothers acted different. They kind of goofed off during the workshops, and at home they acted like it didn't bother them at all that Dad was leaving. After Dad was gone they acted like nothing was different. But if Mom ever mentions Dad's new wife, they get really mad. One time David pounded the table with his fist and stomped out of the kitchen, slamming the door. Mike sort of choked on his food and then glared at the wall. He wouldn't answer Mom when she asked what that was all about.

The boys' room is next to mine. A couple times I've heard noises like someone is crying, but when I go in to check they're both asleep. What I think is they really miss Dad, and it hurts them really bad that Dad would leave them. He only sees us on Christmas and for one week during summer vacation.

nurturing children. For many kids the parent who most often feels overwhelmed in the divorce is Mom. She is often depressed and overloaded, and neglect commonly occurs, despite her best intentions.

Abuse

Whether behavior as routine as yelling at the kids, an act as denounced as sexual molestation of a child, or anything in between, abuse escalates during the stress of marital conflict. Abuse is a parent being mean to a child. It can include yelling at children, harshly criticizing them, calling them names, hitting or slapping them in a passion, letting kids see adult sexual behavior, or actual sexual molestation by the parent. Because of the complex web abuse weaves around the entire family, we often refer to a professional counselor abused teens who hint of their circumstances during the workshop.

During the stressful breakdown of a marriage, adults sometimes regress into inappropriate, abusive behavior. Major fights can erupt, leading a parent to scream at and even hit a teen. Sometimes the kids hit back, and a major fight ensues. We have worked with kids who have been beaten, kicked, and even thrown through glass doors.

Parents who don't yell and hit their kids may abuse them in other ways like not shielding their own promiscuous sexual behavior from their kids. If Mom or Dad bring dates home to spend the night, for instance, they may neglect or refuse to be private during sexual encounters. Some parents even attempt to relate sexually with a child as a way to escape their own feelings of loneliness, fear, and inadequacy.

Overcontrol or enmeshment

In their loneliness or anxiety about divorcing,

Well, I came to the workshop, but I didn't want to. Didn't have no clothes fit to wear in a church. Kevin, my buddy, said it didn't make no difference, and his mom was taking us, and she said if I went she'd pay for me and Kevin to ride the go-carts at the fun center for three rides—one for each night of the workshop. So, hey, I went.

Kevin and I were in the back that first night, but the leader guy came and talked to us anyway. He was all right. Kevin talked the most. I guess I felt stupid being there. I had something left of a black eye my dad had given me a couple days before, and I didn't want to get beat up again, so I hadn't gone home till after midnight and left before my dad got up in the morning. So I probably didn't smell too good, either.

The last night of the workshop I could feel myself kind of breaking up inside. It was like being with friendly people made me feel—well, I don't know. But I told the leader guy that my dad was used to beating on me and that my social worker had sent us to counseling and that Mom had left us a year and a half ago. I don't know why I said all that to him. But I felt better when he knew. Plus some of the other kids in the workshop I see at school. Maybe it'll help.

parents often pursue inappropriate closeness with a young person, displaying emotions that overwhelm the teen, in an effort to manipulate the teen into comforting or taking care of them. Parents may turn to a child instead of themselves or a spouse or friend to meet their primary emotional needs. The parent may overly restrict the child from peer activities as a way of insuring time with the child. Hurting parents also may pursue a best-friend relationship with the young person that sacrifices appropriate distance and authority.

Or in trying to protect a child from the emotional pain and feelings of failure the parents are experiencing, they may smother or overprotect the child. Parents try to make up for the divorce by making everything perfect for the child. When parents respond to the stress of divorce by tightening their control over the children and demanding perfection of them, rules become rigid and school grades and other "performances" become crucial and pressured. It's as if parents try to cope with the failure of divorce by making sure their kids succeed for them.

Dysfunctional modeling

Children learn powerful lessons by witnessing their parents' behavior. The way their parents treat each other is a young person's primary model of what an intimate relationship is like. Unfortunately, children of divorce often see dysfunctional patterns of communication, physical assaults, unfaithfulness, betrayal, deception, and aggressive litigation. It hurts children to see someone they love being hurt. When parents hurt each other, they teach their kids that hurting each other is okay.

The above patterns of pain in divorce—feeling abandoned, neglected, abused, enmeshed, as well as witnessing a dysfunctional marriage—leave children of divorce with powerful pain, fear, and hurt. The bottom-line message they receive through a divorce is that they don't really matter to their parents. They begin to question their own value—"If I were really worth loving and protecting, my parents would stop the fighting and the divorce, because they must know it's tearing me up inside." Since the fighting doesn't stop and the divorce becomes final, low self-esteem emerges in a young person.

Dealing with Gains in Divorce

Most stories of divorce that we hear from teens fit the above painful patterns. Yet that is not the entire picture. Some kids also report patterns of gain—advantages that emerge from the divorce.

Peace and safety

The most common positive report we hear from kids is that divorce has separated them from a troubled, hurtful parent. Kids who with their mother move away from a violent, alcoholic father, for instance, celebrate the relief from his abuse. Even though the separation may not have been easy, the kids say they feel grateful and happy that it's over. We hear this response most often from kids who clashed with a step-parent whom the mom married impulsively. When he's finally gone, they're glad.

For some kids it's not so much separation from abuse directed at them that relieves them. It's experiencing what the kids simply call peace. The war between their parents is over—or at least it's no longer in their face every day. If the battle continues, it happens in the courts or over the phone.

Better parenting

Another gain we hear about a lot is that some parents actually make changes in themselves through the process of divorcing, and after separation they each become better parents to their children. Fathers in particular sometimes make an effort at improved parenting when they are on their own. When they visit their kids they actively listen to them, communicate with them, and enjoy doing things together with them—which is a new experience for many fathers and kids. Some adults value their kids more highly since the kids are "all they have."

Parents sometimes grow personally in ways that can be helpful to kids. They may seek counseling, attend self-help workshops, or go to church. The loss they feel because of divorce may propel them into personal evaluation and both emotional and spiritual growth. They consequently become more mature adults and better parents, models, and companions for their kids.

MOM'S MY FRIEND   Jackie's Story

I used to hate my mom almost as much as my dad. I couldn't understand why she let him treat her like dirt. He'd even beat her up physically. Dad never actually beat me up, but he'd slap me in the face if he was good and drunk, and he'd yell at me whether he was drunk or not.

But Mom started going to a support group for abused wives, and one day she stood up to him and told him to get out. I thought it was about time. The funny thing was, Dad really did get out. What a relief. Mom did all the divorce paperwork, and he never fought it. Mom and I started going to church together, and we heard about the divorce recovery workshop. She went to the one for adults and I went to the one for the kids. Mom's even started going

for counseling at the place where she met with the support group. I really respect her for putting a stop to the abuse and trying to get back into life.

I used to hate to wash dishes or anything, but now Mom and I do all the housework together and then go out to get a pizza or something. Things are tight—both Mom and I work. At least I work when I'm not in school. One thing I have that keeps me going, though, is that we're saving so I can go to cheer camp this year. Tryouts are in April, and I'm pretty sure I can make it. Mom's applying for a partial scholarship for me, too. She never used to be able to do stuff like that. In some ways she feels like my friend on top of being my mother.

Functional families

A final gain that sometimes comes out of divorce is the addition of a positive step-parent and/or siblings through remarriage. Some adults do make better choices the next time around, and some kids do get new families they really like and bond with. Though the percentage is small, this gain is real for those kids.

Gains, however, are often mixed with and overshadowed by the patterns of pain mentioned previously. Kids feel confused that one day they hate the divorce and the next day they are relieved it happened. We try to help kids see that divorce is not black or white, that there can be both gains and pains, and that they can accept their experiences and feelings instead of fighting with them.

Dealing with Changes in Divorce

Divorce brings changes. Among the adjustments that kids must navigate are changes in parent-teen relationships, changes in family communication, and changes in environment.

Changes in parent-teen relationships—the custodial parent

Children of divorce end up living with one parent, called the custodial parent; the other parent becomes the visiting parent. (While the practice of split custodial parenting is increasing, it is still relatively uncommon.) When teens begin to live with a custodial parent (usually Mom), they often take responsibility for the chores Dad used to do—lawn-mowing, taking out the trash, cleaning the garage. And since Mom generally has to start working outside the home, added chores might also include housecleaning, caring for younger siblings, and cooking.

Most teens resent these extra duties, but some feel pride and satisfaction in helping out and gaining more competency. Teens need help to accept willingly some extra responsibility in a single-parent home without having to miss too many of their age-appropriate activities. After-school sports and dating should not be automatically out of the question because of the divorce.

MAN OF THE HOUSE — Bobby's Story

When I first showed up at the workshop I was really mad at my mom—and it wasn't just for making me go there. I figured she sent me so that I would hear about how now that she was alone I really had to help her out. She would even say to me, "You're my little man around the house." Sheesh. I mean, at fifteen, I'm pretty old to be the "little man."

But the humiliation wasn't the worst of it. She made me drop out of soccer at school, and I never had time to do things with my friends on weekends. I said, why didn't she get my little couch-potato brother to do something, but she thinks he too young.

I wasn't quiet about my feelings at the workshop, either. But what everyone said really surprised me. The leaders even told me it was normal and okay to feel mad about the divorce and how it changed my life. And then they gave me some ideas about talking to Mom.

I guess I had been unfair to her, too, because when I did what the leaders said and told Mom how I felt trapped by her and lonely for my friends, she said she understood how I felt. She cried a little and hugged me and said she was sorry, that she had been stressed out over all that had gone on in the last year. Well, then I felt bad for sounding selfish. We worked out a plan for me to work at certain times and have other times for doing things with my friends. It's too late for soccer this year, but Mom says that next year my brother will be able to help out more and maybe I can go out for the team again.

Teens in a single-parent home not only take extra responsibility around the house, they also assume some of the emotional roles of the departed spouse. The custodial parent may lean on his or her children for emotional support, reassurance, affection, counsel, or companionship. While teens sometimes welcome the added closeness in a time of loss and stress, too much emotional responsibility can become an inappropriate burden for a teen to carry, frequently provoking withdrawal on the teen's part and even defiance in response to a perception of smothering.

Teens need help learning how to care about their parents' feelings without assuming a comforter role more appropriate for an adult peer, such as a friend, pastor, or counselor. Brief talks and affection are enough for teens to give their parents. Kids need to learn to express their feelings of discomfort if their parents cross the line from appropriate companionship to smothering dependency.

Changes in parent-teen relationships—the visiting parent

A teen's relationship with a visiting parent (usually Dad) is changed as well. The bond is now based on periodic visits that are often complicated by conflicting schedules, competition, or logistics (where to sleep in Dad's tiny apartment, for example). The bond may be challenged by fear of abandonment, pain of separation (especially when the pair are separated by a long distance), resentment toward him for leaving home, and discomfort and anxiety because of a growing alienation. Teens most successfully overcome problems with the visiting parent when they say plainly

---

A STRANGER AT HOME   Jason's Story

I used to hate going to my dad's every other weekend for my visit. After the divorce he moved to an apartment close to his work, and I didn't know anybody over there. Plus later, Dad got a girlfriend and every time I was over there, she'd be hanging all over him. She even spent the night sometimes. I usually ended up watching TV all day. It was really boring.

A year after their divorce, when I was twelve, Mom made me go to the divorce recovery workshop, and they talked about what to do when you don't like to visit one of your parents—tell them. But I was scared to talk to Dad about what I was feeling. We used to fight all the time when he lived with Mom. Anytime I tried to explain how I felt he would just say, "Who's the father in this family? I said no, and that's final!" But one of the kids in our discussion group told us how she had talked to her mom, and it worked. So I decided to give it a try.

I told him on my next visit that I felt funny when that woman was always in the apartment. He was quiet so long that I finally looked at him. He was making our dinner, and he just stood there with the can opener staring at it. Finally he said, "It's not much fun for you to come over here." I didn't know what to say. It wasn't a question. All of a sudden I felt kind of bad for my dad.

"Well, hey," I said, "maybe we could do something together, just you and me, sometime, like go to a movie or . . ." It was hard to think of stuff you want to do with your dad. But he wasn't mad.

We talk more when I'm over there now. And Dad bought me a couple of framed posters that we hang up behind the hide-a-bed when I come over. It's sort of our tradition now. Also, Judy's only over on Sunday afternoons. She's getting to be okay. And last month Dad bought me a boom box with ear phones so I can bring some of my tapes over. It's like he wants us to get along. This is a different side of my dad. I like it.

what they are feeling and what they want the arrangements for visits to be. Along with asking for what they need, teens must also give and take on the arrangements in light of their parent's needs and limits. We try to help the kids tell the difference between significant needs and changes that they can live without. Things like having their own room with a few of their things at Dad's place, being able to see him without his new girlfriend, or doing things with their own friends while staying at Dad's rank among the significant needs teens should discuss with their parents.

Changes in family dialogue—communication triangles

When parents who separate have a communications breakdown, they commonly convey verbal and emotional messages to each other through their children. There are three ways in which teens get caught in these communication triangles.

As messengers: "You tell your dad for me . . ." followed by an angry message. Threats or messages about money or feelings should be communicated directly between parents or through an adult third party, such as an attorney.

As spies: "Who's your mom seeing tonight?" might be followed by third-degree questioning. Parents may try to garner information about dating patterns, spending habits, moral behavior, and more. Children ought to be left out of any issue that is part of the parents' ongoing warfare.

As dumping grounds: "If you only knew what she did to me. Let me tell you . . ." Many times parents vent their pain and anger in front of their kids. Since teens still need and love both parents, it hurts them when one parent puts the other one down. It can also create loyalty battles for the child, as if each parent is trying to get the child to love him or her most.

THE THIRD DEGREE   Dan's Story

I didn't look forward to returning home after visiting Dad. Mom was still hurt about their divorce, and every time I'd come from Dad's, she'd corner me. It always started out sounding nice. "How was your weekend?" she'd ask. When I'd just say, "Okay," and try to get to my room, she'd follow me. "Did you and your dad do anything special?" No matter what we did, I knew that wasn't what she cared about. "Was it just the two of you?" And then we'd get into the third degree. And she acted so hurt if I didn't tell her, and then she got so hurt once I did tell her—I just hated it.

And if it wasn't who he was with, it was what he had bought. I swear she had an inventory of all Dad took when they divorced. I'd say something harmless like, ". . . so then we watched a VCR and fell asleep on the couch." "You just fell asleep sitting up?" she'd ask. "Well, no," I'd say. "We made it into the hide-a-bed."

"Well, he never felt he had the money to buy us a hide-a-bed. I suppose he bought a matching chair and end table, and then he's crying about not having enough money," and off she'd go.

One of the leaders at the workshop really helped me out. She said I didn't have to tell my mom anything, that it wasn't wrong for me to just tell her I preferred not to talk about Dad's new or old life or what he buys, because it makes me uncomfortable. At first Mom acted hurt when I told her that. Then she got mad when I said it after I got home from Dad's one night. I talked about it in the discussion group at the last workshop, and the kids told me to stick to it. It's hard to say no to Mom, but I can see that it's better for both of us.

The role of intermediary is stressful for teens, because the messages are usually full of intense hostility and distrust. If the parents need a mediator, it is a role better assumed by adult peers or professionals. Teens need help escaping communication triangles.

Petite Amy, a seventh grader, was Mom's money collector. Each visit with her dad on the first of the month was completed only when he handed her the check to bring to Mom. Being the check carrier pressured Amy into feeling resentment toward both parents. On one hand she felt that her mother used her to communicate a subtle message of disdain intended to hurt her dad. On the other hand her dad sometimes put her off and said he would mail the check in a couple days, just to show her mom he was still in control. We encouraged her to let Mom know how pressured she felt and to ask Mom to procure the support money some other way.

Changes in environment

Divorce almost always requires that teens adjust to new homes, neighborhoods, schools, parents, and siblings. They have to get used to how much money is now available for needs and discretionary spending, which relatives they won't be visiting any more, and what's okay to tell the custodial parent about their visit with the other parent (and what will only start a fight) and who their parents are dating. Endings and beginnings abound in this time of transition.

Change, whether good or bad, brings stress. Multiple changes increase stress. And unwelcome, uncontrolled change adds even more stress. Bad stress generates anxiety, fear, fatigue, and the feeling of being overwhelmed. In our workshops we teach kids to recognize the amount of change and therefore the amount of stress that they have in their lives. They brainstorm a list of losses and gains they have experienced because of the divorce. Then we tell them that anyone going through that amount of change experiences anxiety and irritability. We talk about handling stress through proper rest, food, recreation, and, most of all, through dealing with their feelings.

Denial and Shame: Avoiding the Extremes

Two mistakes sidetrack effective divorce recovery for teens: the first is minimizing the impact of the divorce; the second is overemphasizing the experience. Adults minimize the divorce by saying things like, "The divorce simply has to be, so keep busy and don't let it bother you." Some people choose to believe that divorce is no big deal, that kids will roll with the punches, get through the experience, and move on. Parents who won't deal adequately with their own divorce experience often hold this view. They want their children to share in their own denial of the painful effects of divorce. The truth is, divorce is a dramatic crisis that significantly shapes the life of a child.

Overplaying the effects of the divorce is the opposite error. Adults, even Christian leaders, tend to think of a child as ruined or badly scarred by divorce. These well-meaning people perceive split families as key evidence of the decline of our culture. Kids of divorce are thus shamed in a way similar to incest survivors or kids of alcoholics. In our workshops we neither shame the kids nor pity them. We don't use the term "broken," for instance, when we refer to families. Families in divorce are not broken in the sense that they cease to function—they continue to work, love, argue, communicate, celebrate Christmas, and so on. Families are living, breathing entities that require loving care and spiritual nourishment to thrive. Although the impact of divorce is significant, children from divorced families don't deserve to be pitied, shamed, or labeled as hopeless. Children of divorce can and do recover to health and wholeness.

In *Surviving the Breakup*, Judith Wallerstein, the principal investigator of the Children of Divorce Project, describes her study of the effect of divorce on children and teens. This study, which did much to remove the sense of hopeless doom often associated with children of divorce, followed a large sample of children of divorce over a period of several years. By the end of the study period, one-third of them recovered to a normal, positive development. A second third struggled, but seemed to work through to resolution with good and bad times. A final third continued to have significant struggles for years.

So two-thirds of these children of divorce worked through the crisis successfully. Why did many kids do well? Part of the answer is that some intact families can be more abusive and destructive to children than divorced ones. Divorce brings loss and abandonment, but ongoing dysfunctional families bring continuous abuse—emotional, physical, or both—to children. Separation from an abusive or self-destructive adult or family system can actually help a child's development. (Of course, divorce does not always bring the relief of resolution. Some families maintain the pain in the changed family formation.)

Divorce is a big deal, and it hits kids dramatically; but it is not determinative and crippling. Kids can and do deal with it. They grow, learn, and move on—especially when they receive appropriate help and assistance.

Wallerstein's more recent book, *Second Chances: Men, Women and Children a Decade After Divorce*, reinforces the troubling, long-term effect of divorce on the kids she studied. She notes what she calls "sleeper effects" (hidden problems that appear later). Being unable to trust and unwilling to be intimate, experiencing low self-esteem, and fearing failure are some of the significant struggles of these kids later in life. But many kids made significant breakthroughs and growth through the hidden problems as they sought help to confront the issues.

Divorce: A Process Not an Event

Children from divorced families not only need to recover from the impact of the event of a divorce, but from living—often for years—in a painful family system. A divorce usually begins with years of often intense marital discord and family conflict, leading to a separation, the subsequent unraveling of two adult lives, and the establishment of two new family systems. Kids are impacted each step along the process. We are not dealing with divorce alone, but also with the effects of dysfunctional family systems, single-parent families, and blended families. This means the range of issues for kids is broad.

In Summary

Knowing what teens experience and feel because of their parents' divorce helps you effectively walk with a teen through divorce recovery. Kids go through similar patterns of pain—abandonment, neglect, abuse, over-control, and witnessing a failed marriage. But kids are willing to acknowledge gains as well as losses—things like peace, better relationships with parents, and sometimes positive step-families. Divorce brings changes to parent-teen relationships, family communication, and the young person's environment. To be most helpful to teens in divorce, neither minimize nor overplay the effects of the divorce on children, and treat divorce as a process that includes living in a painful family system, the divorce event, and the pressures of the altered family structure. ♥

3
TEENS' EMOTIONS IN DIVORCE: GRIEVING THE LOSS

Randy Smith

Knowing what teens experience in divorce is only half the picture. The other half is knowing the emotional impact of divorce on kids. Since teens experience a wide variety of emotions throughout the divorce process, no one pattern can comprehensively organize those emotions for discussion. In her book *On Death and Dying*, however, Elisabeth Kubler-Ross, physician and psychiatrist, offers a model of six stages in the grief process. With the additional feelings of relief and guilt, I will use her model to explore the emotional impact of divorce on kids.

Before you can compassionately approach young people grieving because of their parents' divorces, though, consider the following attitude toward emotions: "Feelings are neither good nor bad; they simply are." We repeat this saying many times to kids in a workshop to give them permission and support for having their feelings. We suspend judgment of their feelings to keep from silencing kids by criticizing them or shaming them. To work through grief, kids must

---

A NEEDY MOM   Sylvia's Story

I couldn't hardly talk in my discussion group without crying. I felt like I was so emotional all the time. After a couple of minutes I left the group to go to the bathroom because I couldn't stop the tears from coming. One of the women who was helping at the workshop followed me. I didn't want to talk, so I acted like I was trying to find my makeup in my purse. But she came over to me anyway and said, "You look like you're carrying the weight of the world on your shoulders."

Well, that really set me off, and she held me while I cried and cried. For once I felt like I was with someone who was stronger than me, someone I didn't have to be strong for. So I told her how tired I was. I told her I love my mom and dad, and even since the divorce I'm friends with both of

them. I told her how I had tried so hard to get them back together, because I could see the divorce was killing my mother. But I could see Dad's side of it, too. Mom was draining him with all her whining and acting so helpless.

When I got that far in talking to the workshop lady, it dawned on me that now that Dad was gone *I* was the one listening for hours while Mom told *me* all her troubles. And added to her old problems was losing Dad, too. I always tried to comfort her, and for a while it would do her some good. But if I was going to be gone overnight or something she made me feel so guilty for leaving her alone—she'd even do her silent treatment, sort of a martyr routine that she used to pull on Dad.

---

become aware of what they feel, receive assurance that it's okay to have those feelings, and then be encouraged to talk about them. Censure or astonishment on our part pushes kids to turn their emotions inward (suppression).

We believe that emotions in themselves cannot be moral or immoral but are one of God's precious gifts to people. It is how we choose to act on our feelings that takes on the moral quality. Encourage appropriate and constructive expressions of the feelings kids experience by letting them tell their discussion groups how angry they feel about what their parents are doing. Then help them channel their anger into an "I" message and communicate it to the one who has angered them. For example, a boy whose father stood him up on a weekend they had planned to spend together can tell his dad, "I am so mad at you for saying you'd pick me up on Friday and then not showing up." When the boy lets his dad know how he feels, it not only opens up communication between them, but also keeps the boy from taking his anger out in the wrong way (by hitting his sister or being hateful to his mother, for instance).

Helping kids to understand what they are feeling, put a label on the feeling, and talk about it in an atmosphere of support and encouragement heals kids' emotions. Another saying we use a lot is, "Let yourself feel and you will heal." This is a central lesson in literature on grief. Feelings normally pass if they are allowed to happen. An added benefit is that the comings and goings of feelings enrich the life of the individual who allows himself to feel.

In order to help kids grieve through intense and uncomfortable emotions, you also must embrace your own emotions. You can't take kids somewhere you haven't been. Do you judge yourself harshly because of the emotions you sometimes feel? Do you give yourself permission to feel anger, pain, or loneliness? Do you deny your feelings or discount them? Are you uncomfortable with your emotions? Are you afraid of the intense or painful ones? Your attitude toward your own emotions dictates how you'll come across to kids dealing with their emotions.

Dealing with Resistance

Even if we are ready to affirm kids' grieving processes, they may not be ready to begin. Many teenagers resist looking at their experience of divorce. Most of them are not aware that they need to grieve. Parents attempting to bring their teens to a divorce recovery workshop often meet intense resistance from their kids. Bribing or threatening is sometimes the only way some parents can urge their children to come. At the first workshop session, we often joke with the kids about who got the best bribe to come.

We have found, however, that patient, persistent caring breaks through kids' resistance. In a setting where the adults accept openness without censure and where other kids talk freely about their feelings, resistant kids learn to drop their attitude. They see how much talking their feelings out helps them. The student leaders at the workshop model openness about feelings, reassuring new workshop attenders that they will feel better if they acknowledge their need to grieve and to talk about their grief.

The Emotions of the Divorce-Grief Process

Karen's story illustrates the intense emotional pain that children of divorce experience. Anger is another typical response to divorce. In the workshops the kids readily compile a long list of what gets lost in divorce. Separation from a parent is a painful one. Then there are houses, neighborhoods, and friends (if the divorce precipitates a move, which it often does), as well as pocket money and freedom (as they have to help out more). They often lose a sibling who lives with the other parent. Many teens report losing a relationship with their fathers, who

I QUIT CARING   Karen's Story

My happiest memories are when I was five or six. My dad was gone a lot during the week because of his job as a sales rep for a publishing company. But whenever he came home, the first thing he said was, "Where's my princess?" and I'd come running. He always brought me a toy or a book—and then he'd sit with me on the floor to play with it or read it to me. I noticed that Mom was never excited to see Dad. He'd try to hug her, but she always had to do something else first. But since that sent him back to the floor with me, I didn't mind much.

One day, just before my seventh birthday, I asked Mom why Dad had been gone so long this time and if he was going to be home for my birthday. She said she didn't know, but not to worry because we'd have a great party whether he was home or not.

I did worry. It was the most important thing to me to have my dad home on my birthday. My seventh birthday came with the promised party, but no daddy. He called me that night—from two thousand miles away. He said he was sorry not to make my party, but he asked me all about it and promised to send me a present in the mail.

It's seven birthdays later, and we still talk over two thousand miles, and he sends his birthday present. Mom and Dad are divorced now, and I only see Dad at Christmas and sometimes during the summer for a few days. I spent so much time missing him and hoping he'd come home again. But I don't hope any more. It hurts too much to care, so I decided to just quit caring.

---

often withdraw from children because of the divorce. And kids talk about losing certain intangibles such as respect, security, and faith in marriage as a binding commitment. These losses trigger an emotional process called *grief*. Both pain and anger are examples of grief in action. Kids generally go through the following cycle of emotions when their parents divorce.

The Divorce-Grief Cycle

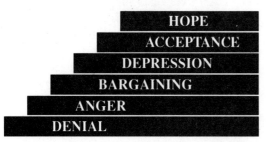

Most kids begin with denial and bargaining, and most end with acceptance and hope, although the order is not rigid, and not every young person feels every emotion. The inten-

sity of the teen's emotions varies with the severity of the family's divorce and with the temperament of the child.

Denial

By refusing to feel or to face the emotions stirred up by divorce, teens in denial can coolly report that they feel fine or at worst numb, as if nothing significant has happened. They can recite the litany of events like a newspaper account, yet show no emotion. When asked what they are feeling, they give replies like, "Nothing, really. It's no big deal," or "Everything's better since the divorce, so I guess I'm feeling okay." They may accept that the divorce is final, but they deny any negative emotional impact.

Three teenage guys sat together in the back row of one workshop, trading comments and quiet laughter. During the break I talked with them and found out they were school friends, each from divorcing families. Their mothers had made them come. All three were casual and cool when I asked about their parents' divorces. They didn't feel that the divorce was a big deal, and they resented their parents making a big deal out of it. Yeah, there were fights and dad's girlfriends and money problems, but that didn't affect them, so they said. They had their fun and their friends.

Sometimes rather than the casual approach, the everything-is-fine kids of divorce stay busy with school clubs or team sports and work to be academic achievers. They look fine on the outside. Achievement, however, may be their protective armor of denial covering over the powerful feelings that are brewing underneath.

Instead of denying the emotional impact of the divorce, some teens deny that a divorce is happening. They see the fights, feel the emotional tension, hear their parents tell them about divorce, and even watch one parent move out. But they discount the events as temporary. Even after legal proceedings are finished, teens in denial may hold onto hope of a reconciliation. These teens attempt to avoid the painful reality of their losses by living in a fantasy in which the divorce isn't really going to happen.

Although denial can be destructive if held on to indefinitely, it is a helpful strategy to delay feelings of loss until kids are strong enough to confront those feelings. Denial, like a shock absorber, cushions the emotional impact of the divorce process, delaying the moment when reality hits. So we don't try to strip the kids' denial away. We talk about what denial is, how it works, why it's helpful for a time. They hear from other kids that divorce impacts all kids, even if they pretend it doesn't.

Most teens eventually acknowledge the reality of their parents' divorce as well as their own feelings about the divorce. Some maintain denial with perseverance, however, sustaining emotional pain that can leave them looking at life through a haze of anger. Sustained emotional pain can show up in a somatic reaction—headaches, stomachaches,

cravings. Or it might lead to chronic depression and low self-esteem. Denial is a helpful first way station, but a terrible destination.

Anger

Most teens, at some point, show their grief about their parent's divorce by getting mad. The changes forced upon their world hurt and confuse them. They lose things and relationships they really want, and it is all happening beyond their control.

Expressions of anger vary with each teen. Angry teens can give sharp retorts to parents or siblings or surly responses to complete strangers, act grouchy with no apparent reason, and interpret the merest suggestion as a sharp rebuke and blow up at the teacher or parent who spoke to them. A young person who is usually cooperative at school may begin to defy the teacher. Anger is often at the root of irresponsibility in completing schoolwork or chores. Teens may express anger by smoking in secret, by purchasing records and posters that model rebellion and anger, or by changing their hairstyle and appearance. Some kids begin fist fights with siblings or kids at school.

Some teens move through anger quickly; others hold on to anger for years, developing deep resentments that repeatedly destroy new relationships. A bitter teen can become a bitter adult.

Although it's hard, you can best help teens through anger by letting them talk their anger out. Angry teens need support and acceptance of their anger. That means you listen to them tell how they feel—"I hate my parents They're just showing me that they don't love me at all." You show support and acceptance by responding with something like, "It sounds like you're really angry right now," or "When you feel like you're losing something important to you, you feel mad."

Yet, inappropriate, aggressive, or self-destructive means of expressing feelings must be confronted. Let kids know you accept their feelings as valid, but that it's not appropriate to express those feelings by beating up a sibling or taking drugs, for instance. Tell them that although they can't always choose their feelings, they can choose what to do with them. The purpose of the workshop format is to create an environment in which teens can vent their feelings and hear about appropriate ways to grow through their situation. We let the kids vent, but we also call them to responsibility and self-care.

Bargaining

In grieving divorce, many teens adopt a temporary emotional strategy called bargaining. Bargaining is testing the reversibility of the loss. Kids try to bargain using their own behavior. "If I can just be perfect maybe Mom and Dad will stay together." They might try the role of peacemaker, urging Mom and Dad to talk together, to work things out, or to seek help. Undermining a parent's relationship with a third party or setting up their own parents to date is bargaining behavior. Some teens deliberately cause trouble at school or defiantly disobey at home in hopes that their parents will stay together in order to handle them. They can even make themselves ill, hoping that Mom and Dad will have to get together to take care of them.

Bargaining is normal—most of us test a loss to make sure it is final and unchangeable. But like denial and anger, bargaining should only be a way station on the road to healthy emotional resolution. Teens need to acknowledge that they are powerless to fix their parents or resolve their parents' conflict. They need to accept their limited roles as children.

Depression

The sad, heavy feeling of emotional pain called depression occurs when teens hit emotional bottom in realizing the extent of the loss

---

I LITERALLY MADE MYSELF SICK — Susan's Story

At thirteen I was very self-conscious. So once I finally agreed to go to the divorce recovery workshop, I only observed and listened. At least that's what I did for the first two workshops I attended. When it was offered again at a nearby church, I psyched myself up to talk. I told my small group that even though my parents had been divorced for two years, I was sure they were going to get back together. I told them how I had set them up to date each other and that I had even talked them into going to counseling—although they hadn't stuck with it. I wanted them to agree with me that it was possible for them to remarry each other.

The kids not only didn't share my hope, but they told me I needed to quit hoping. "You just don't know how I feel," I started to say angrily. I caught myself in time. They did know. I felt really hurt and embarrassed that I'd said anything. But Cindy, my student leader, caught me before I left and asked if we could get together and talk some more.

She took me out for a milkshake after school on Thursday. I told her about how lately I'd been missing school because I had stomachaches so bad. Mom even had to stay home from work. And a couple times Dad had to come over and stay with me because Mom couldn't get off. Mom and Dad both were talking about taking me to the doctor.

Cindy told me that it would be good for me to see a doctor, but she suspected that I might be making myself sick by so urgently wanting my mom and dad to get together. After we talked the pieces fit in my mind—I knew she was right. Later I called my dad to tell him what Cindy had said. He thought she was pretty smart. He came over that night, and both he and mom sat down with me to tell me that the divorce could not be reversed and that they didn't want it reversed. I could see it was best to let go of my hope for their remarriage to each other, even though it made me sad to give up my dream.

I was a small-group leader for the workshop that Joshua, a junior high boy, attended. His mother had recently left him and his dad to be in another relationship. Right away I could tell he was hurting, but he didn't seem ready to talk with the rest of the kids. He sort of slouched down in his chair with his arms folded and looked right at whoever was talking.

The week after the second workshop I called him to see if he wanted to get together for a Coke at McDonald's after school. He said okay, and I picked him up at school. We talked about school and football teams and what a hassle it was getting homework done. I was waiting for Josh to make the first move. He didn't—

not then, anyway.

On the final evening of the workshop, Joshua really unloaded on the small group, telling us how much it hurt to have his mom leave and how angry he was at her. When he was done talking, he took a deep breath and then blew it out again. It was like with that breath he cleaned himself out of some heavy emotional dirt. Some of the kids in the group said it would go better for him if he told a couple of his friends at school what was happening at home. He looked a little skeptical, but he saw the evidence right in front of him. There were a couple of kids who had been through divorce and had made it by being willing to talk it out.

before them, the irreversibility of the divorce, and their helplessness to change it. "This is happening to me and I hate it. It's the pits."

Depressed teens might withdraw to their rooms, watch television, bury themselves in music, or just daydream. They may cry or mope, or just lose interest in life and having fun. Some indulge in eating, shopping, or using alcohol and drugs to escape their feelings. Others manifest depression by always being busy or by staying with friends to escape their own family's conflict.

Often the most risky stage, depression leaves teens vulnerable to abuse—more open to drug dealers or sexual abusers. Some teens feel they'd rather be dead and display suicidal gestures at this point. Depressed teens need extra care, support, and watching. You can ask their student leaders to call them or take them out to lunch, or encourage one of the other kids to invite them over.

Periods of painful sadness are inevitable for most kids of parents in conflict, and they need to be allowed to walk this road. In other words, don't feel you've got to encourage a kid out of the blues. It's healthier to let it run a course and run out of steam. Depression doesn't have to

be severe or dangerous, especially if teens get emotional support. Whereas you need to help an angry teen master his angry responses quickly since anger is such a powerful emotion, a depressed teen is more in need of support while working through the depression. If a teen stays in depression for longer than three months, however, it's time to recommend intervention counseling. Depression that is severe or long-term can be serious.

A teen who is in depression often won't seek out support. You need to approach those who appear withdrawn, on the edge of tears, high on a substance, or unkempt. Let them know that someone cares by asking them questions about what they're feeling. Your concern allows them to trust you, and they begin to open up and share. If any teens seem seriously depressed, we recommend counseling to them and their parents.

Acceptance

No one can reach acceptance without working to some degree through the other grief feelings. Teens who let themselves grieve and feel emotions like anger and depression will eventually be ready for acceptance. Acceptance is a feeling of peace and calmness, of being okay with what is. Teens who reach acceptance choose to let life happen on life's terms, not their own. They realize that "What will be, will be"—they can't change things. Acceptance means admitting powerlessness over others and events. Kids need to be encouraged to accept the divorce when they are at the right place in their grief—when they have acknowledged their parents' divorce, accepted it as the way life is now, and openly talked out their emotions of anger and depression. Acceptance for teens is not a happy place, but it is a place of peace.

Hope

The goal of the grieving process is hope. Hope means seeing some daylight after a long, dark tunnel. It means that even though the divorce has been painful and tragic, some of the losses are being offset by gains. Replacing the losses is an important part of establishing hope. During the last session of the workshop, the kids make a list of gains. After the lost schools or neighborhoods are grieved, teens begin enjoying the new ones, which bring new opportunities and friends.

Many report better relationships with parents who, free of the old fighting, put more energy into being good parents. The kids say that from their parents' divorce they learn a lot about what does and does not make relationships work. They report learning to handle difficult feelings, and they gain self-esteem through their hard work as survivors. Some come to really like new stepparents and stepsiblings. Although many remaining losses will hurt for years to come, recognizing gains brings hope to many.

Relief

No matter where they are in their grieving process, kids commonly mention feeling relieved once the divorce is finalized. They often say things like, "I'm just glad it's over," or "I'm so happy that the jerk moved out."

Relief feels like happiness—a lightheartedness that comes when a burden has been lifted, a suffering ended, or a pain removed. When divorce finally physically separates quarreling parents, lessening or eliminating intense verbal or physical conflicts in their home, kids commonly perk up for a time, relieved at the cease-fire after an exhausting

---

GROWING THROUGH DIVORCE — Sheila's Story

My brother Bob and I have had a long time to get over Mom and Dad's divorce. It's been seven years now since they split up. We were lucky enough to have an older couple in our church sort of adopt Mom and us after the divorce. It was so easy for Bob and me to talk to them about what we were feeling, and they helped us sort through our hurt and anger.

We all still feel sad that the divorce had to happen, but it wasn't the end of our world after all. At first we thought it was. But I can say truthfully that I really like Mom's new husband. He tries hard to be a friend to me and to show me he cares about what I am doing and how I am feel-

ing. He came to at least half of my gymnastic meets this year—and that meant leaving work early to be there on time. That means a lot to me.

Bob isn't as close to him as I am. I guess because he was older when Mom remarried. But he and our natural dad get along better now than they ever did before the divorce. They work out together after school at the gym. Dad never used to have time to do that kind of stuff.

Both Bob and I feel like we've grown stronger in our relationships with God through the trial of divorce. We learned that we had to put things into God's hands.

war. Now parents fight over the telephone or in the lawyer's office, not in front of the kids. Physical separation can also mean the removal of the parent who may singlehandedly be making the family's life miserable, ushering in peace and relief.

Like denial, relief is a rest stop on a long, painful journey. Let kids feel relieved. Affirm their focus on the gains of divorce, gains like peace in their homes and growing closer to their custodial parents. Relief is a normal, appropriate feeling that they can embrace and talk about. Some kids fear that if they express relief, their parents might feel the kids wanted the divorce to happen. Assure them that you understand the reason for their feelings of relief, and that it is not wrong for them to feel relieved. Relief is one of the easy feelings that accompanies a divorce and will probably be replaced by more exhausting emotions that are also important parts of the grief process.

Guilt

Many kids assume guilt for their parents' divorce. They torment themselves with questions like, "Did I misbehave? Did I try hard enough to help Mom and Dad?" Kids who have relied on bargaining behavior often think they have failed their parents when the marriage fails. This inappropriate guilt is usually caused by poor emotional boundaries (ways of being healthily separate) within a family. The parents either overtly or covertly make the children feel responsible for the parents' emotional happiness.

Teens can also feel intense guilt if they side too much with one parent in the divorce. Without meaning to, parents often increase their children's guilt load by playing emotional tug-of-war with them—confronting them with questions like, "Who do you think is to blame for the divorce?" "Which parent do you want to be with?" and "Don't you think your father is wrong to leave?" Teens can feel guilty even for expressing their own feelings about the divorce.

Kids need to know that they are in no way responsible for their parents' divorce. They do not need to accept the guilt they may feel or the guilt that a parent may put on them when they say things like, "The divorce was my choice, of course, but your bad behavior sure caused a lot of fights between Mom and me." It is our belief that children are never the cause of divorce, even though parenting them may be a significant conflict for the adults. It is the adults' rigidity, immaturity, or poor choice of partners that precipitates divorce.

Encourage kids to let go of guilt rather than assume responsibilities that are not theirs. Teach them that the feeling of guilt is a healthy check when one's actions violate one's values. But the actions of young people are not responsible for their parents' decision to divorce. Although kids can't change their parents, they can learn to change themselves and ultimately to trust God with the rest of the family.

In Summary

Divorce requires significant adjustments of a young person's life, producing stress and initiating an emotional cycle of grief over loss. Teens' reactions to divorce vary in intensity, but usually follow a pattern of shock and anger that stimulates bargaining and depression and ends in acceptance and hope. Teens can feel a peaceful relief, but they often have to deal with false guilt.

All six of the feelings in the grief cycle, as well as relief and guilt, are normal emotions experienced by teens going through their parents' divorce. Kids need to experience them to some degree to truly resolve the divorce and its impact on them. The quickest way out of these feelings is to walk through them. ♥

4
CARING MEANS PREPARING: THE COMPETENT YOUTH WORKER

Stephen Murray

You are willing to help others, but are you able? When Randy and I reflected on our experiences in youth ministry, we noted that any success we have enjoyed is the outcome of high-quality information delivered through significant relationships, resulting in our personal transformation. We've been taught how to live, both temporally and eternally, by gifted teachers, pastors, writers, and speakers. Through supportive friendships and loving mentors we continue to grow in our knowledge and love of Jesus Christ. We see the Holy Spirit work in us and through us. Within these relationships we test and validate our knowledge. These associations expose our fears and insecurities, our immaturity, arrogance, ignorance, and hardness of heart. They smooth our rough edges and rejoice when we make progress in the things of the Lord. Thus we are being transformed.

Teens going through divorce also need to receive high-quality information delivered through significant relationships in order to be transformed. This means that along with knowing what they are going through and providing them with helpful information, you must be personally linked to the Lord, to a local fellowship of believers, and to other youth workers. Walking teens through divorce recovery is more than a one-man job. Your preparation for a ministry of divorce recovery must include a deliberate commitment to increase your knowledge continually and to build and maintain healthy relationships.

Your Need for a Ministry Network

Your church staff, volunteer leaders, fellow youth workers, and other community resources are essential to you. A qualified Lone Ranger is a myth. Teens in crisis often need specialized care, and you need a network to help you discern when a teen needs that kind of care and how to provide that care. If you suspect that a teen is considering suicide, for example, you need the counsel of someone trained in recognizing the symptoms of teenage suicide. For the legal protection of yourself and your church, you need to communicate with your senior pastor on referral cases. In order to make effective referrals, you need to be acquainted with the local suicide crisis-intervention center as well as professional counselors.

Accountability to superiors and ministry peers, and readiness to refer needy kids protects and better equips you. Such sharing of responsibility gives you support and prevents you from getting in over your head.

Bob, a highly motivated and hard-working youth worker who felt tremendous empathy for the problems of teens in his group, had a lot of deep emotional needs of his own. Since he had never discussed them with anyone, he had no peer who could assure him that these were valid needs that could be addressed through counseling and the prayerful support of others. Bob's subsequent affair with a counselee might have been over before it began had he been linked to a caring network of youth workers, colleagues,

My dad was an alcoholic when I was growing up, and me and my two brothers did our best to help Mom make ends meet. I went to church, but it wasn't the kind of place where you could talk about problems. Mostly I felt like I could only talk about spiritual successes with my youth leaders, and the preacher spent a lot of time talking about "victorious Christian living."

I got a lot of affirmation in the youth group, because I was outgoing and liked to ham things up. During high school I struggled with loneliness and feelings of inadequacy, but felt I might lose my leadership position if I told my youth pastor about how I was feeling. One time I did try to tell him what was going on, but he just told me to pray about it. I got the message that I shouldn't have problems, or at least shouldn't talk about them.

I felt best when I had a girlfriend and was in the limelight at church. I was also eager to help other kids, since I knew how tough it could be at home. I went to college knowing that I wanted to be in full-time ministry. Looking back, I realize that I didn't have any close friends and that I really needed to be needed by others in order to feel any self-worth.

After finishing college and seminary, I began working full-time as the youth pastor in a mid-size congregation. Counseling with teens was my favorite aspect of the ministry. I gave the counsel and support I would have liked to have received when I was a kid. I could really identify with the kids' hurts and fears and their need to be accepted. It was especially easy to get close to the girls, since they were so much more in touch with their feelings than the guys.

Kristin, a girl in my youth group, drew out my compassion. Her dad, like mine, was an alcoholic. For about two years I counseled her through some rough times, including several failed relationships with older guys. She let me know she was interested in something more from me, and I let her know I wasn't. But that eventually changed.

I was struggling with my feelings toward Kristin, but I didn't know who to talk to. I was afraid to talk it over with my pastor in case he might lose respect for me and question my ability to handle the job. I met regularly with some other youth workers in the area. We often kidded around about this sort of situation, and now I was too embarrassed to admit that I was facing it. I decided to just pray about it and stop seeing Kristin.

Kristin came by my house one evening, and I told her that we could no longer see each other. When I broke the news to her, she started crying and told me how much she loved me. Then she embraced me. As they say, the rest is history. She and I got involved. The kids in the group found out about it, as did their parents, and the church eventually asked for my resignation.

Well, my relationship with Kristin ended, and I am now picking up the pieces of my life. Professional counseling has helped a lot, as has the support and love I have felt from friends. Their love and support was always there; I just couldn't receive it. I realize now that I had an unmet need for love and affirmation that I didn't know how to cope with. And I wouldn't discuss it with anyone for fear of being rejected.

At this point I don't know if I will ever have a ministry again. But I do know one thing, I need the help of others in order to deal with my weaknesses and temptations. I wish I could have learned this lesson another way.

and friends with whom he could share his life.

As an associate pastor, I belong to a covenant group of peers with whom I feel free to share my weaknesses, temptations, and needs. I am privileged to be on a church staff whose practice is to log in with each other concerning personal struggles and ministry challenges. I am close to several ministry colleagues with whom I can share my need for direction, support, guidance, and wisdom. I would rather be embarrassed as I share a need for help than to have to sift through the wreckage of my own (or someone else's) life down the road. Too many Christian leaders are going it alone. The situations encountered in working with emotionally needy people demand a strong support system for the care-giver.

Especially veteran youth workers, who have seen, heard, and done it all, are vulnerable to moral failure and burn-out. The rugged individualist is an enduring stereotype in all forms of ministry, but burn-out is usually the cost for excessive self-sufficiency. Satan's strategy is primarily one of divide and conquer. The failure of many men and women in ministry is the result of first succumbing to the temptation to go it alone. The consequence is to rust-out, fade-out, poop-out, fizzle-out, drop-out, or crash-and-burn-out. We are members of a body, designed to function in association with our fellow members.

Your Personal Growth Toward Wholeness in Christ

We are, all of us, wounded healers. Our own experiences with pain and loss sensitize us to the pain and loss of others. While we can never fully enter into another's pain (and neither would it be wise to try and do so), our own season of recovery equips us to empathize with others and perhaps be more helpful to them. (Henri Nouwen's *The Wounded Healer* is an excellent reference for what it means to help others.)

I can remember my own pain at seeing my parents suffer a rocky and destructive marriage.

I also had many problems with my father, both during and after adolescence. Some of these painful feelings I have come to terms with; other feelings are still in process. Although I worked through the grief of my mother's sudden death, I still feel her loss on certain occasions. I am not perfect, but I am in the process of growing into wholeness in Christ.

Take a long look at your personal experiences with pain and loss. Can you accept them and work with them? Remember the rule: Feelings are neither good nor bad—they just *are*. What you *do* with your feelings can be evaluated as good or bad. Where is your growing edge emotionally? Spiritually? When people resist personal growth, they risk becoming dispensers of pat answers and cliches.

Three words have captured my attention as I am growing into wholeness in Christ through ministering to children of divorce: authenticity, vulnerability, and integrity.

Authenticity

Authentic people recognize and accept imperfection in themselves and others. They realize that, by the grace of God, they are in process and will one day be found complete in Christ. In the meantime they allow others to see them as they really are, warts and all. Authentic people don't represent themselves as authorities on divorce, for instance, but rather as people who care enough to initiate a healing encounter.

Work at coming alongside teens in a way that will neither embarrass nor intimidate them. Don't approach kids in a group and announce to one of them, "Hey, I heard your folks are getting a divorce." Respect their privacy. Throw out feelers when you catch a kid alone for a moment. Tell him you know his folks are having a tough time and you want to let him know you're available to talk. And don't wear your pastoral role like a badge that makes kids want to be careful what they say in front of you. Let them sense from you that feelings are okay and that you're able and willing to hear them out.

Teenagers are willing to be vulnerable to an authentic—as opposed to a faking—adult. Kids are self-protective and suspicious of adult attempts to pry into their psyche. They know from experience that many adults tell kids "how it is" or help them in ways that feel more like emotional intrusion. Authenticity allows you to demonstrate genuine concern for a young person, to communicate the Lord's love to him. Professional therapists call that kind of love "unconditional positive regard." It means that you don't demean kids by seeing them as helpless little projects. The way you talk and the expressions you wear tell them, "I see you as a person of dignity who's going through a tough situation."

You may have had the uncomfortable experience of trying to talk with a teenager, only to have the encounter turn into an interrogation/interview routine that leaves you feeling frustrated. Authenticity helps you to earn the right to get close to a young person. It might take some time for kids around you to be certain you have it.

Vulnerability

A "willingness to feel" begins to describe a vulnerable person. Vulnerable people experience deep emotions because they allow themselves to do so. Exposing your true self, allowing others into your life, entering into the pain of a teenager who struggles with a promiscuous mom or a new stepparent—these are the experiences of a vulnerable person.

Being vulnerable—staying in touch with personal weakness, pain, self-pity, anger, hopes, and dreams—equips you to treat each teenager as a unique, unrepeatable miracle of God's handiwork rather than as a project or case study. Remaining vulnerable allows you to identify with teens whose stories are similar, but who still need you to empathize with them individually. Vulnerability is the opposite of becoming hardened to what others are feeling, without going to the other extreme of living on nerve endings.

You may perceive yourself to be an unemotional person because you do not express your emotions outwardly. But it may simply mean that you need to develop effective and appropriate ways to convey your feelings to others. Our *affect* (our facial expressions and body language) can reveal or hide what we are feeling.

Being vulnerable is risking no one coming to your workshop, having people misunderstand your theology, or worse yet, having people understand your theology and reject it. Overly self-protective people insulate themselves from self, from others, and from the Lord—from risk. A friend gave me the following poem when he heard me talk about risk:

To Risk

To laugh is to risk appearing the fool,
To weep is to risk appearing sentimental,
To reach for another is to risk involvement,
To expose feelings is to risk exposing your true self.

To place your ideas, your dreams before the crowd,
Is to risk their loss.
To love is to risk not being loved in return.
To live is to risk dying.
To try is to risk failure.

But risk must be taken,
Because the greatest hazard in life
Is to risk nothing, do nothing, be nothing.

He may avoid suffering and sorrow,
But he simply cannot learn, feel, change, grow, love or live.
Chained by his attitude, he is a slave.
He has forfeited freedom.

Only a person who risks is free.

Reprinted with permission of Nightingale-Conant Corporation from *Living, Loving, and Learning*, by Leo F. Buscaglia, PhD. Copyright 1988 by Nightingale-Conant.

Integrity

Integrity has to do with being of one piece, whole and complete—demonstrating unity between what one says and does. Determining to live with integrity means choosing a process of coming together rather than coming apart. In other words, we need to walk our talk, provide stable examples of single or married life, teach the Scriptures with conviction, and minister the grace of God.

Many young people lament their parents' flakiness in moral and ethical matters. Divorce seems to exacerbate this lament. "Does anyone around here do what is right instead of just doing what is easy?" they ask, and rightly so. Though none of us is entirely consistent, hopefully we can be depended upon to point the way to what is true, right, and good. I cannot minister effectively to teenagers if I am not personally responsible for my life. Teenagers caught in the midst of separated, divorced, and blended families need to see role models of integrity.

Because we are spiritually integrated, we want to help people where they are, with no strings attached. Like the good Samaritan, we are simply trying to love our neighbor in a way that honors God. This means we do not use divorce as an excuse to manipulate people into the kingdom of God or to prey on a young person's impressionability.

Being a person of integrity also means resisting the impulse to talk people out of what they are feeling or thinking about their divorce experiences. Integrity demands that I allow a young person to be angry, confused, frightened, skeptical, or disinterested. Integrity holds in check my need to be needed, liked, listened to, admired, and respected. My role is to give freely what I have to offer and trust the Lord for the outcome. The Holy Spirit is the source of my integrity; only as I allow the Holy Spirit to work with me and through me will a teen be able to benefit from what I have to offer.

Being a person of integrity means not promising too much. "This workshop is going to change your life and solve all your problems" should not appear on your promotional brochures. A counseling session or a work-shop doesn't remove all the pain of everyone who attends, but it can teach young people how to understand and process pain to some degree. When teens understand their pain, they can manage it constructively.

When you make promises you are dealing with your own needs and securities instead of the kids' needs. Saying, "I just know if you forgive your dad you're going to feel so much better," tells a kid that you're so uncomfortable with his feelings that you'll promise him just about anything to get him to change those feelings. Rather, talk to them about moving toward dealing with their anger by talking it out, for instance, instead of acting out. Share your observations and experiences of life without giving advice. Let them talk themselves into perceiving their own needs for change.

Finally, integrity means offering young people hope rather than hype. One girl wrote to me following a workshop, "I have recovered from my parents' mistakes, and I continue to succeed on my own. I've learned to like the independence, but I still have battle scars." At another workshop a girl, who had participated in two workshops and was now a discussion-group leader, approached me during the break with tears in her eyes. "I feel like a failure," she said, "because after three workshops I am still not handling my feelings of loss over not having my dad involved in my life." I couldn't promise her freedom from emotional pain and I didn't minimize her feelings by telling her not to worry. As we talked I helped her realize that her loss is real, and the painful feelings it started come back now and again, even though she has started to grow through the events of the divorce.

In Summary

The process of personal transformation in Jesus Christ that happens in the context of accurate knowledge and a healthy network of relationships is the foundation upon which effective ministry is built. You not only need support and accountability, but you must be willing and able to draw on your own experiences of recovering from pain and loss in order to effectively minister to young people.

Teens respond most readily to an authentic, vulnerable person growing toward integrity in Christ. ♥

5
HELPING TEENS BY COUNSELING THEM

Randy Smith

Adolescents don't necessarily want to or know how to deal with feelings. From the ages of twelve to fifteen, the repression of feelings is natural and designed, because this growth stage presents intense and overwhelming feelings. While some repression is functional, kids in divorce need help acknowledging their feelings, especially when they are grieving. If kids let themselves feel and deal with what is happening inside, then they can grow and learn from loss and endings.

But the feelings of kids experiencing divorce are especially intense, and a caring adult friend can play a key role in divorce recovery for teens. Teens in conflict often need people outside their families to whom they can ventilate confused feelings without getting lectured, criticized, or punished. They need guidance and support from someone who can help them through painful, important choices. They need support in facing a difficult situation or relationship.

The Caring Helper

Teens often resist talking. If a teen meets your words with hesitancy or moves in and out of topics, build rapport by walking, eating, or relaxing together before coming back to the topic. Respond to reluctant teens with patience and perseverance. Initial resistance to a caring helper is normal. Teens talk to the people they choose, and then only at certain times. If a teen doesn't choose you, let go of it and encourage her to connect elsewhere. It's nothing personal; it's simply the teen's choice. If you are the right person at the right time,

God has opened a door—thankfully step through it.

Here are four qualities that will help you make the most of an opportunity to counsel a teenager.

Focused attention. Good counseling begins with good eye contact and a warm, open posture. Your physical presence demonstrates that, for the moment, you have consciously set aside your other agendas and cleared your mind to be there for this teen.

Showing interest. Pointed opening questions like, "Tell me what's gone on in your family," or "What's it been like for you in the divorce?" invite a teenager to talk about his experiences and feelings. Initiating communication with him shows you're interested and concerned.

Supportive listening. Reflective comments ("That must be hard," or "Sounds like you're pretty hurt") or comments that feed back your feelings ("I feel sad, too") let teens know that you heard them. Listening without offering advice, judgment, or your own stories demonstrates your acceptance of their feelings. When kids feel acceptance after sharing, they are encouraged to share more. Talking lets them examine what they are experiencing and move through their feelings to a place of acceptance and hope.

Offering help. To be attentive, interested, and supportive earns you certain rights—the right to ask deeper questions, to help kids explore things more deeply by confronting them, to tell them how what they say affects you, or to offer problem-solving suggestions.

If you're the kind of person who wants to "fix" kids, you may be tempted to offer problem-solving suggestions too quickly. If, on the other hand, you fear turning kids off, you may be tempted to avoid giving specific advice. With good timing you may be able to offer support ("You are not alone. I am here, and so is God"), forgiveness or hope ("You are not responsible for the choices your parents are making"), a confrontation ("You are expressing your anger aggressively and really hurting your family and yourself"), or a suggestion ("Try talking honestly with your mom about that—maybe she really cares"). The bibliography of further reading found in Appendix E lists books that can give more in-depth and clinical approaches to counseling teens.

Specific Strategies for Intervention

What can you give teens to help them cope well with divorce? Steve and I try to help them learn four main skills: dealing with feelings, learning negotiation, being responsible for myself, and reaching out to God.

Dealing with feelings

Our first objective is to teach teens how to move through the grief process most effectively by dealing with feelings in healthy ways. The model we use for approaching the powerful feelings of grief teaches three options: take it out, hold it in, or talk it out.

Take it out. The first option is the aggressive approach of dumping on others—impulsively expressing anger by yelling, hitting, screaming, name-calling, or even intense and manipulative crying or self-pity. Teens can dump on their families (usually singling out a "safe" or weaker parent or sibling), peers, or authorities outside the home (teachers, for example).

Taking feelings out on others is a destructive option that hurts others and violates their right to be treated well. Teens who dump on others have a hard time getting the support and sympathy they really need because they so often make others angry with them. While it is not always wrong for kids to blow up, we encourage them not to choose the "take it out" option, though most will fall into it at times. Sometimes blow-ups allow kids to let others know what they are really feeling (even if they don't blow up in the most mature way). But kids can be guided to approach issues with less volatility and more appropriate self-control.

Hold it in. This second way of dealing with feelings is bottling—never talking about or expressing feelings. Bottling often includes withdrawal, pouting, vegetating, silent self-pity, passive-aggressive behavior (expressing anger by holding back approval or love), avoiding responsibilities, and even anesthetizing or avoiding emotions through over-absorption in television, music, fantasy, and other escape mechanisms.

The hold-it-in approach prevents self-growth by not letting others know about important emotions, such as anger and depression. Bottling makes a person self-centered and self-absorbed. Internalized anger and sadness can harm the body, causing stress-related symptoms such as susceptibility to flu, colds, headaches, and ulcers. Those who bottle things in might become compulsive about food or drugs in order to suppress and medicate their feelings. This option can lead to suicidal feelings and even attempted suicide.

Bottling is a destructive way of dealing with feelings, and we encourage kids not to choose it. It is not always wrong, however, to hold things in and think about them. Teens need privacy and space at times to work things through. But there should be a balance. They also need to talk.

Talk it out. Choosing this healthy and functional option allows teens to express—with assertion, honesty, and openness—what they think, feel, need, and want. They describe their hurt and anger instead of dumping or bottling. Although they may not say things calmly and nicely, or structure their expressions by perfect assertion-training standards, the important thing is that they can let others know their inner responses to outer changes.

An assertive approach to sadness and depression, for instance, is to allow one's self to feel sad, talk, and even cry with a trusted friend. When people talk out their feelings, they move through depression and hostility to hope. We all learn and grow when we allow ourselves to experience our pain and other feelings—otherwise, we may remain stuck in depression and hostility.

Learning negotiation

The second skill we attempt to teach teens in divorce is to negotiate with parents. Negotiation is trying to resolve conflicts through communication and compromise rather than either avoiding confrontation or forcing one's own choice upon others. Teenagers are prone to flee from conflict, give up on parents, or just do what they want.

Negotiation is simple in nature, involving four basic problem-solving skills:

Identify wants. When you support teens and accept their feelings and wants, you help them to have the self-confidence they need to find out exactly what they feel, need, and want.

Express wants. The next step is to help them plan a clear, reasonable, and respectful way to present their points to parents, neither hiding what they want nor being aggressive.

Be willing to compromise. Encourage flexibility and compromise (give and take). Try to teach teens that in the reality of life, most of us don't get all that we want, but that some is better than nothing at all.

See the other side. Finally, help teens see their parents' perspectives on things. Such

guidance can help teens accept decisions that don't go their way.

Issues that need to be negotiated vary from chores and responsibilities to money, time, and rules. If a teen wants money, we encourage her not only to ask her parents for it but to offer to help out more in exchange. If she wants more weekend time with friends, we encourage her to ask her parents to extend more trust in exchange for responsible behavior away from home (honoring the curfew, for example). These exchanges build trust and are the essence of negotiation. When teens approach their parents with openness and willingness, parents often respond in turn with flexibility and trust.

Being responsible for me

The third skill we teach teenagers is to take responsibility for understanding who they are and for letting others know what they need and want. Responsible teens acknowledge their power to make choices and recognize that their choices will make a difference. Responsible teenagers are learning to value the unique and special people that they are—often in spite of put-downs or losses that they experience because of the choices of others. Young people who think of themselves as valuable are more motivated to be responsible.

Taking responsibility also involves setting goals, deciding to pursue healthy and satisfying things in life, doing well in school or sports, caring for friends and family, and doing happy, enjoyable things. We are responsible to treat others well and care for the needs and feelings of the important people in our lives. We are not, however, responsible for others, and their needs should never dominate and control us and become our own. We can care about others—we cannot carry them.

Reaching out to God

Many young people come into our workshops without faith in God, with bitterness towards God, or distancing themselves from God. Sometimes the teens have hard questions

One thing I've learned being a small-group leader at workshops is that kids want to hear other kids' stories. The lectures are great. And every time I go I understand something a little better. But what really makes the difference for a hurting kid is hearing what other kids have gone through and how they made it.

So I was telling this new kid Pete how when I first came to the divorce recovery workshop I was a wreck. I felt so mixed up, and I was so mad at my parents for destroying my life that I basically struck out like a cornered animal at anyone who tried to help me. But I came to the place where I could see it wasn't helping me or anyone I liked to be so hostile. I was, in fact, doing to other people what I was so mad at my parents for doing to me—I was unloading into their lives all my immaturity and selfishness.

Well, Pete didn't say much, but he came to church with me a couple of times. Our youth group did an overnight camp-out in the mountains and he came along. At the Saturday campfire our youth pastor told his own story about meeting Jesus. It really woke something up in Pete. On the ride back home it was just me and Pete and our youth leader in the front of a pickup, and Pete asked question after question about Jesus and about being saved and what that was like and how you did it.

At a rest stop we pulled over so we could pray, and Pete received Jesus as his Savior. I felt really great being in on that. We even joked about baptizing him in the water fountain like Philip had baptized the Ethiopian in Acts. I have seen Pete trust God through bad times. It really made me realize what a difference Jesus can make when a person lets him do his thing.

about God that we try to help them with. As fellow-strugglers we let kids know our experiences with a God who has reached out and cared for us—even in the toughest of times. In a workshop setting, student leaders also tell stories of how God has helped them through it all. We encourage attending church as a key way of getting closer to God, and we let kids know what kinds of activities our church offers. Personal invitations from student leaders often draw hurting kids into the group.

Referring for Counseling

At times some teenagers need more intensive help or help of a different kind than you can give in a workshop setting. Let them know that when they are really hurting or struggling, it's okay to ask for help. Tell them that pastors and therapists are there for support and guidance when they need to talk, and tell them how to contact one. At our workshops we stress that if they have worked on a problem like depres-

sion, drugs, or fighting with parents, yet they still feel stuck, then it is time to ask for help. We have on hand, if a request is made, the names of Christian therapists with appropriate training, licensing, and experience.

In Summary

A caring helper gives a teen focused attention (physically and mentally), shows interest by asking questions, responds with reflective and supportive comments after listening, and offers affirmation, suggestions, guidance, confrontation, and hope. Through lectures, small-group discussions, and one-on-one talks, teens are stimulated to talk honestly about their feelings, to negotiate the stressful changes in their environments, to take loving responsibility for themselves, to act responsibly toward others, and to reach out to God. In encouraging these skills, we help teenagers grow through—instead of merely go through—their parents' divorces. ♥

SECTION TWO

THE DIVORCE RECOVERY WORKSHOP

HOW TO USE THE WORKSHOP SECTION

In the following section, which contains everything you need to know to do a divorce recovery workshop, you are assumed to be the workshop coordinator. The entire workshop section is your coordinator's notebook. Certain clearly marked, reproducible pages should be used to create the notebooks for your workshop leader, workshop host, and your student leaders. Any pages not clearly marked for inclusion in a staff member's notebook are for your reference, or you may pass them on to another helper in the workshop.

Near the front of this section are three tables of contents for you to use as you organize individual notebooks for the basic workshop. Instead of organizing by page number, these tables arrange the necessary portions of this book as they will be needed by various staff. For example, the group discussion questions appear in the host's notebook under recruiting and training student leaders, because the host only uses them during the student-leader training session. On the other hand, these same questions appear in the student leaders' notebook near the outlines for the sessions in which the student leaders will use them.

Appendix A contains all the forms you need for the basic workshop. Appendix B contains the information for the one-day workshop, including the agenda and any other reproducible pages distinctly related to the one-day workshop format. The details of the lectures, discussions, and skits are the same as for the basic workshop, so that information is not repeated in Appendix B. Neither are any of the forms in common repeated.

Appendix C contains the information specific to the Friday night/Saturday format of the workshop. Appendix D contains the information specific to the weekend-retreat format of the workshop. It contains an added lecture on forgiving, to be given at the Sunday-morning session.

If you plan to conduct a workshop using one of the formats detailed in the appendices, use the tables of contents from the basic workshop as models and create tables uniquely suited to the workshop you have chosen.

Appendix E contains a list of books for more in-depth study of the subject of counseling teens.

The information needed to flesh out the lecture outlines in the workshop is found throughout Section One of this book. Although the instruction in Section One and the following workshop material equip you with everything you need to know to present a divorce recovery workshop, it is not designed as a read-as-you-go program. We've learned this information in bits and pieces, through reading and experience, by talking it over and listening to feedback. The danger in our putting it all down so neatly for you is that you'll be deprived of the benefit of having searched for information, picked out ideas significant to your own objectives, tried them, refined your approach, and committed your experience to writing so you can remember how you did it. All of which means that the workshop leader will need to digest Section One to effectively offer the lectures or conduct the discussions.

Just as the workshop leader needs to own the material to effectively present the workshop, the student leaders who assist in workshop chores and discussion leading need to own their material. The more time the workshop coordinator spends preparing the student leaders, the more the student leaders will assume the responsibilities and the attitudes of leaders—authentic leaders, regardless of their age—who serve the participants.

The various agendas for the workshop are suggestions. They are not the only agendas that work, but are guides for your workshop planning. Consider the Rhodes family skits to be guides as well. During rehearsal and even during the presentation of the skits, the student leaders can enhance the script with actual dialogue that they recall from when they were going through the various stages of grief. Or they can emphasize the point of the episode (dealing with anger or bargaining or acceptance) by exaggerating their performance.

Workshop | Leader

Host

Student | Leader

WORKSHOP LEADERS'
TABLE OF CONTENTS

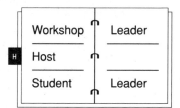

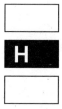

HOSTS'
TABLE OF CONTENTS

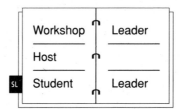

STUDENT LEADERS'
TABLE OF CONTENTS

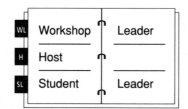

ADOLESCENT DIVORCE RECOVERY WORKSHOP: PREMISE AND GOALS

Let's begin by looking at the workshop title, Adolescent Divorce Recovery Workshop, which clearly states both the premise and the goals of a workshop.

Adolescent

Although the workshop is appropriate for junior-high through college-age young people, the majority of participants are thirteen to eighteen years old.

Divorce

The workshop deals specifically with the issues adolescents face when their parents separate or divorce, including the problems of single-parent and blended families. Since the breakup of their parents' marriage is only one factor in teenagers' lives, however, participants also discuss problems in areas such as studies, sports, friends, dating, and other relationships. Several activities are geared to help them accept responsibility and build their self-esteem.

Recovery

People need to *grow* through divorce rather than simply go through it. Recovery implies taking charge of one's life and moving ahead into healing and wholeness.

Some teens feel little need for recovery, since their parents divorced when they were too young to know what was going on. Other teens are proverbial basket cases and can hardly speak in the workshop without weeping. Their felt need for recovery is keen.

Nevertheless, all teenagers benefit from the workshop because it helps them identify and empathize with some of the issues their parents have faced. In addition, teens are at a point in life when they draw conclusions from their experiences and apply them as strategies for living. The workshop allows teens to process this data, reflect on the experience, compare experiences with other teens, and integrate vital new information into their world view.

Workshop

A workshop is the single most effective vehicle for helping teens grow through divorce. In this holistic learning experience, group participation draws teens into mutual interaction, support, discovery, and growth, while respecting the individual's privacy. The leaders' genuine enthusiasm and interest encourages kids to buy into the experience. Yet it is not the leaders' workshop; it belongs to the participants. The kids own the process by actively participating in it. Thus we must not treat them as case studies, objects of pity, or people who need to be straightened out through our Delphic utterances.

This workshop is designed on the principle of planned spontaneity. Neither the activities nor the lecture are scripted word for word so they will be fresh, not canned. The workshop functions best when adept leaders facilitate a dialogue between themselves and the kids. Leaders become adept by adequate preparation and experience.

CONSIDERING ADOLESCENT NEEDS AND DEVELOPMENT WHEN PLANNING THE WORKSHOP

The developmental realities of adolescence have definite implications for the workshop:

Physical

Teens can't be expected to sit for two hours of lecture, so we do a mixer, take a refreshment break, move into small groups, and do role plays.

Cognitive

Teens need to be challenged intellectually. We are careful to avoid oversimplifying the issues. Young people resent anyone talking down to them—or talking over their heads. Psychological concepts must be communicated in a way that interests them and lets them see the application to their situations.

Affective

Although intensely introspective, young people often hide their feelings behind a poker face. For most kids, the workshop provides a safe outlet for them to express and deal with their feelings about the separation, divorce, or new family. Talking out their feelings initiates catharsis and growth. But some young people have so carefully buried their feelings that the workshop at best spurs them to get in touch with their feelings again. The workshop content is balanced between head and heart to accommodate, integrate, and process a wide range of thoughts and feelings. Using humor throughout the sessions loosens the kids and leaders up so they aren't overloaded when confronting heavy issues.

Moral

Many kids begin a workshop with a strong sense of moral outrage. Probably eighty percent of them come from homes where a third party has been the cause of the marital break-up. Although many of these teens accept pre-marital sex as permissible, they have strong convictions regarding extra-marital sex and its accompanying deception. To them it is clearly wrong. While respecting their point of view, morally mature workshop leaders help the kids explore these moral dilemmas and shore up their moral framework.

Social

Most kids perceive a divorce recovery workshop as socially embarrassing. They don't like to appear needy, and going to this workshop indicates a sense of need. Some kids are still rebelling against the divorce or against a parent. For them, coming to a workshop means cooperating with the enemy! We diffuse these feelings during the first session by finding out who was bribed into coming to the workshop (and for how much). The kids love it because they can laugh about the crazy lengths to which their parents have gone in order to get them there. This approach lets the kids know we are aware that this can be a socially uncomfortable situation.

The mixers break the ice, but the student leaders and small-group work provide the social glue that holds the workshop—and its participants—together. Social contacts established in the small-group sharing time and a personal note from a caring leader bring kids back for the remaining sessions.

Ironically, a few kids who really get into the program do not return for the sake of winning a battle with Mom or Dad. Usually, though, participants brought to the workshop by parental fiat continue because they like it. The typical rate of attrition is about five-to-ten percent over the course of three sessions. Some

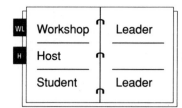

students must drop out because of scheduling problems with school, sports, or work.

Spiritual

All teenagers are spiritually hungry. We tell the kids that we sponsor the workshop because God's love motivates us to do so. Although we emphasize the relational/transformational nature of God's love, we see the workshop not as an evangelistic tool, but rather as first aid for wounded people. Some kids have become Christians through their participation in a workshop, but many of the kids are already believers. For most of the participants, we are cultivating the ground and planting seeds for a later harvest in their lives.

Personal

Personalities are shaped by three factors:

- Genetic makeup—inherited from Mom and Dad.
- Significant others—people who influence one's life.
- Life experiences—environmental influences.

In addition to these factors, teens are living through a critical developmental period that extends from early adolescence through late adolescence. Thus, although they share the life experience of divorce or separation, workshop participants display a wide range of needs, strengths, and weaknesses, because of the many other factors influencing them. This means you'll have to look past clothes, hairstyles, mannerisms, and other outward symbols that may mask the needs within.

Workshop | Leader

Host

Student | Leader

MAKING THE BASIC WORKSHOP HAPPEN

Overview of the Workshop

The basic workshop is divided into three two-hour sessions (7:30 to 9:30 p.m.) scheduled one week apart. The general outline of all three sessions is:

- Prayer with leaders before participants arrive.
- Greeting and registering participants.
- Mixer.
- Lecture and skits.
- Refreshments.
- Small-group discussions.
- A different activity for each session.
- Session summary.
- Debriefing of student leaders.

Offer the adolescent divorce recovery workshop in conjunction with an adult workshop, if possible. That way, you'll have a pool of potential participants for the adolescent workshop. You can also join the adults for a potluck supper to begin your third session. (For more information on the adult Divorce Recovery Workshop, write to the Singles Ministry Resources, P.O. Box 3010, Colorado Springs, CO 80934, or call 719/579-6471.)

Time Line

3–12 months ahead
  Schedule the workshop dates, set a budget, and recruit the workshop leader, coordinator, host, and secretary.
4–8 weeks ahead
  Recruit student leaders.
4–6 weeks ahead
  Develop a brochure or flyer.
2–4 weeks ahead
  Distribute the brochures or flyers.
1 week *after* workshop
  Send thank-you notes to all workshop staff.
2–3 weeks *after* workshop
  Adult leaders hold "Thank-You Brunch" for everyone who helped in the workshop, especially the student leaders.

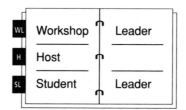

JOB DESCRIPTIONS

Staffing

An effective workshop requires people who can fill the following staff positions:

- *Coordinator*

  This volunteer person (or couple) oversees the entire workshop from planning to completion. The coordinator works with the host to recruit and train student leaders and other staff, orders supplies, and fills in any gaps in the workshop arrangements.

- *Workshop Leader*

  This individual makes the majority of presentations during the workshop. Ideally the workshop leader is a Christian counseling professional who relates well to teens and is an effective workshop presenter. The workshop leader may need to be licensed, depending on your state laws. This experienced marriage and family counselor, clinical psychologist, or psychiatrist is also able to refer participants for psychological help, if necessary, and is prepared to deal with issues such as child abuse or substance abuse that may surface during the workshop. The workshop leader may also help train the student leaders.

- *Host*

  This youth worker participates in the workshop and provides continuity between the workshop staff and the sponsoring church or school. The host welcomes the participants every week and leads the mixers. The host helps train student leaders and debriefs them at the end of each session. The host might also serve as workshop coordinator in a pinch.

- *Student Leaders*

  This group is the key to a successful workshop. They should be mature young people who

  - are in college or their last year of high school.
  - have experienced divorce in their families.
  - can relate well to their peers.
  - show concern for others.
  - commit to training and all sessions.
  - are teachable and open to feedback.

  Student leaders are responsible for preparing refreshments, greeting and registering workshop participants, leading small-group discussions, and sending personal notes to participants after the first session, encouraging them to return.

- *Secretary*

  This person assembles materials, sends out letters, reserves the workshop room, arranges for it to be set up, and so on. (These duties may also be handled by the coordinator or host.)

Workshop | Leader

Host

Student | Leader

BUDGETING AND PUBLICITY

Budgeting

Usual costs include expenses for items listed below:

- Honorarium for the workshop leader.
- Dinner for the student leaders.
- Session refreshments (brownie mixes, etc.).
- Stationery and postage for follow-up letters to participants.
- Promotional flyers.
- Other promotional items (T-shirts, for instance).
- Miscellaneous supplies.
- "Thank-You Brunch" for workers.

To finance the workshop, a sponsoring church may offer a contribution from its youth budget, or if you are offering it in conjunction with the adult workshop, perhaps some of those funds can be used.

Publicizing

- If your workshop follows the adult workshop, add information about the teen group to their flyers, brochures, or other publicity.
- If you're on your own, create a brochure for the teen workshop to include with your monthly or weekly church mailing and to place in community centers or the YMCA.
- Create a poster announcing the teen workshop. Distribute copies to churches, youth centers, community bulletin boards, and schools around town. Consider placing newspaper ads and asking for free public-service spots on your local radio or TV stations.
- Design T-shirts with the divorce recovery logo (p. 109) on the front and the slogan, "Don't just *go* through it, *grow* through it," on the back.
- Include the following information on all your publicity:
  - ☐ The workshop name and place (a map is helpful).
  - ☐ The time and all three workshop dates.
  - ☐ The names of the workshop leaders.
  - ☐ The cost of the workshop (or that it is free of charge).
  - ☐ The deadline for registration.
  - ☐ A brief paragraph describing the workshop and inviting teens to come whether their parents are divorced or separated, recently or long ago.

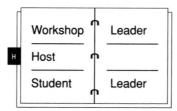

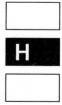

ORGANIZING THE WORKSHOP SESSIONS

Physical Arrangements

Here's a checklist to help you get organized:

☐ Select a room large enough for the participants to divide into small groups, but not cavernous (such as a large gym for a workshop of twenty people). Or arrange to use several adjacent rooms, one of which is large enough for the entire group to meet together.

☐ Provide chairs for everyone, arranged in a circle or horseshoe and facing away from the door.

☐ Place one table by the door for registration and another table at the back of the room for refreshments.

☐ Request a chalkboard and possibly a podium for the workshop leader.

☐ If you anticipate a large group, rent or borrow a sound system with a microphone and cassette tape deck. Background music helps participants relax, as long as it doesn't intrude.

☐ Lay out name tags and marking pens.

☐ Make several copies of all four kinds of registration sheets (Appendix A).

Providing Refreshments

The coordinator purchases brownie mixes, apple juice, milk, paper cups, and napkins out of the workshop budget. At the leader-training session, student leaders sign up to prepare the brownies and bring them to each session.

RECRUITING AND TRAINING STUDENT LEADERS

Recruiting for the First Workshop

Select several qualified young people to invite to be student leaders. In a personal letter to each of them, describe the workshop and the student-leader training session, and tell them the dates for both the workshop and the student-leader training. Briefly describe the responsibilities of a student leader and ask them to return an enclosed application form if they are interested in being a student leader for the upcoming workshop.

Once you receive the filled-in applications (follow-up with a phone call when teens are slow to respond by mail), interview each potential leader. Call those you select to be on your leadership team and then send them a letter congratulating them on their selection, reminding them of the dates, and inviting them to the leader dinner and training session.

Recruiting for Subsequent Workshops

At the end of each workshop, file the names and addresses of those participants you feel would be effective leaders-in-training. Before the next workshop, send them a letter inviting them to apply. After helping with one workshop, the trainees become full-fledged student leaders.

Send your experienced student leaders an invitation to participate again. Many student leaders volunteer year after year. Eventually you may have to ask them to sit out a workshop to avoid burnout! (All forms and sample letters for the basic workshop are in Appendix A.)

Scheduling the Leader Dinner and Training Session

Plan the leader dinner and training session to take place about a week before the workshop begins (on the third night of an adult work-shop, if possible) from about 7:00 to 8:30 p.m. Invite the student leaders, leaders-in-training, workshop leader, coordinator, host, secretary, and everyone else who has a hand in offering the workshop. Send everyone a postcard reminder (or call them) a few days before the training.

Preparations for the Leader Dinner and Training Session

- Plan a simple dinner, such as take-out pizza or hamburgers (The fellowship group at the church may be willing to lend a hand).
- Buy as many brownie mixes as you think you will need for refreshments at all three sessions.
- Make several copies of the advance-registration sheet to take to the adult workshop (Appendix A).
- Write up name tags ahead of time for everyone attending the training session.
- Prepare a three-ring notebook or folder for each student leader with the following handouts:
  - ☐ *Student Leaders' Table of Contents* (p. 63).
  - ☐ Outlines of all three sessions, containing current workshop dates (pp. 85, 86, 87).
  - ☐ *How to Be a Better Listener* (p. 91).
  - ☐ *How to Lead a Small Group* (p. 92).
  - ☐ Lists of discussion questions for each session (pp. 93, 94, 95).
  - ☐ Sample letter for student leaders to send to workshop participants after Session One (p. 96).
  - ☐ Scripts for the Rhodes family skits (pp. 97–107).
  - ☐ Add any other handouts you feel will be helpful for the student leaders.

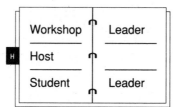

Agenda of Student-Leader-Training Dinner

6:00 p.m. Welcome, introductions, and dinner.

6:30 Prepare your student leaders for the workshop (see below).

7:30 (Optional) Attend an adult workshop to introduce your leaders, briefly explain the adolescent workshop, and ask the adult participants to send their kids. Encourage them to bribe their kids to come, if necessary. Pass around the advance-registration sheet so the parents can indicate how many kids they will send to the adolescent workshop as well as the ages of the kids.

7:45 Return to your meeting place to practice the Rhodes family skits and make assignments for the workshop.

Preparing the Student Leaders

Give each student leader a copy of the notebooks you have prepared. As you discuss the areas listed below, ask the leaders to refer to their own copies of the italicized items.

- *Premise and goals*. Briefly examine the philosophy behind the workshops.
- *Staffing*. Discuss the roles of the workshop leader, coordinator, host, and secretary. If those people are present, invite them to explain what they'll do at the workshop.
- *Greeting*. Participants may be in unfamiliar surroundings and feel uncomfortable just being at the workshop. The student leaders can help them feel welcome—but not by attacking them with killer friendliness. A warm smile and a question or two about where the participants live or go to school will do it.
- *Registering*. Show the group copies of the four categories of registration sheets (Appendix A).
- *Session outlines*. Overview the content of each of the three Session Outlines.

- *Leading small-group discussions*. These discussions are the most important part of the workshop. At the first session you will assign a team of two student leaders to each group. An ideal team consists of a boy and a girl, one an experienced student leader and one a leader-in-training, both the same age. At the first session you will assign each team a small group of participants who are the same age or younger than the team. Participants will remain in these groups with the same student leaders for all three sessions.

As the leaders follow on their copies of *How to Lead a Small Group*, discuss the points listed there. Your student leaders may feel nervous about leading a small group for the first time, so encourage questions. Talk through *Small-Group Discussion Questions* to give them a feel for leading a discussion. Using *How to Be a Better Listener*, remind them to set an example of good listening during all sessions. If you have time, ask two volunteers to demonstrate good listening.

- *Follow-up note*. After the first workshop session, student leaders will write a short note to the participants in their small groups. Review the sample letter in their notebooks to show them how short and simple it can be. Explain that at the end of the first session you will provide writing paper, envelopes, stamps, and the addresses of the kids in their groups.

- *Session One details*. Ask the leaders to turn again to the *Outline of Session One* in their notebooks. Go over it in more detail, stressing ways you expect the student leaders to help. Urge the leaders to become part of the group by sitting among the participants rather than clustering together. This will avoid an us-versus-them dynamic. It is extremely important that the student leaders mingle with the partipants and give them the feeling that we're all in this together.

- *Rhodes family skits*. Assign the four parts for the Rhodes family skits: Mom (Marie),

Workshop Leader

Host

Student Leader

Dad (Matt), Susan (14), Eric (10), and Robbie (6). Explain that the skits are discussion starters for the workshop participants. They are most effective when the kids assume a distinct personality for each part. Susan, for instance, might use a valley girl dialect, and Eric might be a skater-dude who always has his skateboard with him.

Robbie could be done in "Little Nemo" style. Hang a sheet in a doorway or another usable spot, placing a table in front of the sheet. One student leader stands behind the sheet. Another student stands in front of the sheet. The student leader in front puts a pair of little kids pants over his arms and puts his hands in a pair of tennis shoes. The person behind puts her arms under the bottom edge of the sheet to be the arms for the Robbie character. The student leader in front reads the lines, while the student leader in back gestures.

Although the kids will *read* their lines at the workshop, they should practice their parts several times before each workshop to become familiar enough with the dialogue to be able to ham it up some.

Making the First Assignments

Here is a checklist of assignments you need to make at the end of the training session:

- [ ] Assign several student leaders to be greeters and two or three others to be registrars and to fill out name tags.
- [ ] Ask for volunteers to bake brownies for each session and distribute as many mixes as you think you'll need.
- [ ] Assign all student leaders to two-person teams.
- [ ] Ask one or two older leaders to use the registration lists on the first evening to divide the participants into small groups by age. (The procedure is described in more detail under *Presenting Session One* [p. 75].)

Conclude the training session about 8:30 with prayer for one another and for the teens who will be attending the workshop. Remind the student leaders to bring their notebooks to each workshop session.

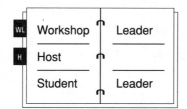

PRESENTING SESSION ONE

Overview

7:20   Adult and student leaders pray together.

7:30   Assigned student leaders greet teen participants as they arrive and help them register.

7:45   Host welcomes group and leads *People Bingo* (instructions on p. 88).

      Assigned student leaders divide participants into groups (instructions below, "Dividing Participants into Groups").

7:55   Workshop leader offers lectures and student leaders present skits on the first two stages of grief: denial and anger (lecture outline begins on p. 76).

      Workshop leader conducts a discussion on *Dealing with Mom* (discussion outline on p. 77).

8:30   Refreshment break.

8:45   Workshop leader conducts optional sharing time (suggestions for sharing on p. 77).

9:00   Student leaders guide *Small-Group Discussion I.* (Discussion begins at 8:45 if sharing is omitted. Student leaders use discussion questions from their notebooks.)

9:25   Closure and invitation to Session Two.

9:30   Adjournment.

9:35   Ten-minute debriefing period with student leaders (p. 78).

Preparing for Session One

Things coordinator needs to buy, make copies of, or gather:

☐ Five small, wrapped candies for each participant.

☐ Milk, apple juice, paper cups, and napkins for refreshments (Student leaders should be bringing brownies).

☐ Stationery and stamps to give to student leaders for their letters to participants.

☐ Name tags for everyone, plus markers.

☐ Four categories of participant registration sheets.

☐ Extra paper and pencils for dividing participants into groups.

☐ List of student-leader teams.

☐ Modify *People Bingo Sheet* (p. 122) as instructed on page 88 and make copies of it.

☐ Pencils.

Dividing Participants into Groups

The assigned student leaders divide the participants' names into small groups while the participants are involved in the mixer and other activities. The larger the workshop attendance, the more age categories you can have; for example, you could group seventh and eight graders together, ninth and tenth graders together, and so on. Ideally, each group should have between five and eight members, with an equal number of boys and girls. Ask the student leaders to give the group lists to you, marked by ages, so you can assign each group to a team of student leaders who are at least a little older than the participants.

LECTURE OUTLINE: DENIAL AND ANGER

I. Introduce the workshop.

A. **Why are you here?** The common bond of all who have come is their experience of divorce and their need to learn how to deal with it. Some may not want to be here, but ask them to keep an open mind and try it out. Ask how many were bribed to come and what their parent(s) offered them.

B. **Will you *go* or *grow* through divorce?** Point out that they can go through their parents' separation or divorce—or they can grow through it. If they choose to deal with it, share their experiences, and learn from others, they can get help and even learn a lot. Divorce is hard, but teens can gain even from difficult times.

C. **Divorce brings loss.** Compare the loss experience of divorce with other losses: the breakup of a dating relationship, death of a relative, even moving.

II. Explain the grief cycle.

A. **Grief is an emotional response to loss.** Describe grief as a series of feelings in a somewhat predictable pattern. The emotions are denial, anger, bargaining, depression, acceptance, and hope.

B. **Face your feelings.** Grieving because of something you've lost is normal. Your feelings are natural and need to be accepted, not feared or judged. It's best to face these feelings and talk about them.

III. Discuss denial, the first emotion in the grief cycle.

A. **Denial feels like shock or numbness.**
   • This isn't happening to me.
   • It won't last; my parents will get back together.

B. **Denial is a protective emotion** that shields you from pain, just as shoulder pads and helmets protect athletes in a football game.

C. **Denial looks different on different people.** It can simply mean avoiding talking about the divorce, or always keeping busy, never slowing down enough to feel or talk.

D. **Denial is okay—for a while.** Denying that something bad is happening gives you time to absorb the loss. But sooner or later a person must face what is really happening and break through the denial.

E. **Student leaders present *The Rhodes Family: Denial*.** Discuss how Susan, Eric, and Robbie each showed denial.

IV. Discuss anger, the second emotion in the grief cycle.

A. **What is anger?**
   1. **We feel anger** when someone hurts us, frustrates us, or takes something away that we value.
   2. **We show anger** in many ways, from passively withholding ourselves to actively

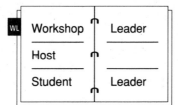

screaming.

3. **Anger is normal and appropriate**, but it can be expressed in destructive ways.

B. **Describe three ways to deal with anger** (and all other emotions to be discussed in this workshop).

1. **Taking it out on others.** This aggressive way of dealing with anger includes hitting, screaming, cussing, accusing others, putting them down, damaging property, and so on. This approach is destructive, tends to hurt others, and resolves very little. Aggressive anger is often directed at "safe" objects, such as younger siblings and friends.

2. **Holding it in.** You can passively bottle your feelings by not talking about them. Anger still comes out in pouting and withdrawing as the person tries to punish others, but it usually hurts the angry person most.

3. **Talking it out.** This is the assertive option, honestly and openly telling others that you feel mad. You can be animated and loud, or soft and reasonable. When we talk out our anger, we move through it and don't stay angry so long.

C. **Student leaders present _The Rhodes Family: Anger_.** Discuss how each child in the story showed anger.

V. Dealing with Mom.

A. **Discuss some of the changes and conflicts** in living with Mom as a single parent. This can include:
- Assuming new responsibilities.
- Having less spending money and less free time.
- Having less contact with Dad—and perhaps with Mom, too, if she assumes a new job.

B. **Learning to negotiate with Mom**, rather than acting out angry frustrations or giving up, is a significant skill. Here are some specific suggestions that may help participants deal with Mom (and other conflict situations):
- Think of what you want and feel.
- Make your request/point clearly and respectfully.
- Be flexible and willing to cooperate.
- Try to see Mom's side of it.

VI. Sharing Time (optional).

A. **Explain** that adolescence is a time of breaking away and strong feelings. Divorce can intensify these feelings, yet many young people feel there is nothing to be gained by saying, "I'm hurting. I need help." Instead, they hide their feelings.

B. **Ask** the following questions, encouraging participants to respond in any of three ways:
- By answering the questions quietly in their minds.
- By sharing their thoughts with the larger group.
- By discussing their answers later in the small groups.

1. **Did you ever ask yourself**
- What did I do wrong to cause these problems?
- How can my folks do this to me?
- What do other people, especially my friends, think about me now that my parents have separated/divorced?
- How could I help Mom and Dad get back together again?

- Will I be okay in the future?
- How are my parents going to change as a result of the divorce?

2. **Have you ever**
   - Had to "become" the missing parent?
   - Lived with a "super parent"?
   - Lived with a parent who is dating?
   - Lived with a stepparent?
   - Lived with stepbrothers or sisters or half brothers or sisters?
   - Been involved in counseling or peer counseling?

Debriefing of Student Leaders

Immediately after the session, spend about ten minutes talking with student leaders about how things went in the small groups. Use their feedback to help plan the next workshop. Here are some typical debriefing questions for all three sessions:

- How did you feel about this session?
- How did you feel about your discussion group?
- Did any unique issues come up in your small group?
- Should we do anything differently in the next session?
- (for the third session) Would any participants in your small group make good leaders for other workshops?

At the end of the first session, distribute stationery and stamps so student leaders can write short notes to the people in their small groups. Be sure to give them the participants' addresses. One way is to make several copies of the registration sheets and give them to the appropriate student leaders.

After both the first and second sessions, briefly review the activities for the next session, which are outlined in the student leaders' notebooks. Be sure to remind those leaders who volunteered to make brownies for the next session to do so.

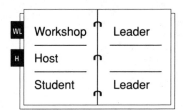

PRESENTING SESSION TWO

Overview

7:20   Adult and student leaders pray together.

7:30   Assigned student leaders greet teen participants as they arrive, register any new people, and assign them to groups.

7:35   Host welcomes group and leads *Slogan Game* (p. 89) and *Good, Clean Jokes* (p. 88).

7:45   Workshop leader offers lectures and student leaders present skits on the next two stages of grief: bargaining and depression (lecture outline begins on p. 80).

         Workshop leader conducts a discussion on *Dealing with Dad* (discussion outline p. 80).

8:15   Refreshment break.

8:30   Student leaders guide *Small-Group Discussion II* (using the list of discussion questions included in their notebooks).

8:50   Workshop leader and student leaders organize *Family Sculpture* (p. 81).

9:10   Host moderates an interview with a teen and parent (p. 90).

9:25   Closure and invitation to Session Three.

9:30   Adjournment.

9:35   Ten-minute debriefing period with student leaders.

Preparing for Session Two

1. Invite a teenager (perhaps one of the student leaders) and his or her parent to be interviewed by the group during this session. Select a pair that is willing to answer questions and share in a positive way how they are learning to grow through divorce.

2. Things to buy, make copies of, or gather:
   - ☐ Milk, apple juice, paper cups, and napkins for refreshments. (Student leaders should be bringing brownies.)
   - ☐ Name tags for everyone, plus markers.
   - ☐ Participant registration sheets from Session One.
   - ☐ List of assigned small groups and student leaders from Session One.

LECTURE OUTLINE: BARGAINING AND DEPRESSION

I. Introduce the second session.

   A. **Ask for feedback**. Thank the young people for returning and ask for comments from Session One.

   B. **Review.** Ask volunteers to name the two emotions you talked about at the first session (denial and anger).

   C. **Preview.** Explain that tonight you'll discuss the next two emotions in the grief cycle: bargaining and depression.

II. Discuss bargaining, the third emotion in the grief cycle.

   A. **Bargaining means testing** whether something is open to negotiation or reversible.

   B. **Young people often try to negotiate change** or interfere with the divorce in some way, the same way they might bargain about household chores.

   C. **Bargaining can include** trying to get parents to see a counselor, attempting to act as a mediator, or even getting sick or becoming a problem to get parents to work together.

   D. **Bargaining doesn't work in a divorce** because it's the parents' decision.

   E. **Bargaining is okay for a while**, but young people need to move on and face the divorce.

   F. **Student leaders present** *The Rhodes Family: Bargaining*. Discuss how each child in the family uses bargaining.

III. Discuss depression, the fourth emotion in the grief cycle.

   A. **Depression is the deepest pit** in our journey of grieving—a sad, heavy, "down" feeling when we realize our loss.

   B. **Depression shows itself in many ways:** we may cry, withdraw, lose interest in fun or work, lack energy, think about problems over and over, stop eating or overeat, have trouble sleeping, or sleep all the time. Some people get so busy and active they never slow down and face the problem.

   C. **Medicating depression** by using drugs, alcohol, or sex, is one way many people deal with their feelings.

   D. **Depression should be talked out,** even with tears, rather than holding it in, taking it out on others, or medicating it.

   E. **Suicidal feelings sometimes accompany depression.** Encourage anyone who has suicidal feelings to get help right away. Name some resources in your community that offer counseling.

   F. **Student leaders present** *The Rhodes Family: Depression*. Discuss how each child in the family shows depression.

IV. Dealing with Dad.

   A. **Discuss some of the challenges** faced in relating to a visiting parent, usually Dad. The

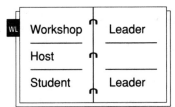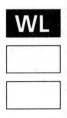

result often takes one of two forms: Disneyland Dad or Deadbeat Dad.

1. **Disneyland Dad** tries to appease his guilt by constantly showing the kids a good time or buying them things. Encourage participants who have dads like this to tell Dad they just want some quiet time with him.
2. **Deadbeat Dad** does very little when the kids visit and often has chores waiting for them (taking over Mom's duties). In this case, encourage kids to be honest about wanting to have some fun and not just clean up.
3. **Participants need to make a place of their own at Dad's,** where they can keep a few personal things and make it feel a little more like home. Tell them to be honest if at times they would rather go to a special activity with their friends than visit Dad.

V. Family Sculpture.

To begin this activity, have a volunteer student leader assign other volunteers (leaders or participants) the roles of the volunteer's family members. Each role play will have three acts:

Act One: My family before the divorce

Act Two: How the divorce happened

Act Three: My hopes for my family

For each act, the leader explains what happened and the actors play it out. After the group understands how *Family Sculpture* works, ask volunteer participants to come up, select other volunteers, and sculpt their own families. This activity helps participants realize that other families experience the same confusion and pain as part of divorce or separation. The role plays generate chaos, laughter, and sadness as the kids recount fights, affairs, and surprises.

PRESENTING SESSION THREE

Overview

(This schedule assumes your workshop is presented in conjunction with an adult divorce recovery workshop.)

6:20   Adult and student leaders pray together.

6:30   Student leaders greet teen participants at potluck supper. (Supper includes teens, adults from divorce workshop, and leaders from both workshops. Kids sit together.)

7:10   Adults and students are invited to share what their respective workshops have meant to them so far.

7:30   Teens go to their workshop. Workshop leader hands out 3 x 5 cards and pencils for participants to write out questions for the upcoming panel discussion.

7:35   *Family Sculpture* (optional; see p. 81 for details).

7:50   Workshop leader offers lectures and student leaders present skits on the last two stages of grief: acceptance and hope (lecture outline begins on p. 83).

        Workshop leader conducts a discussion on *Keeping Out from Between Mom and Dad* (discussion outline on p. 83).

8:20   Refreshment break.

8:35   Student leaders guide *Small-Group Discussion III*.

9:00   Host moderates panel discussion (p. 90).

9:25   Participants fill in workshop evaluations (Appendix A).

9:30   Adjournment.

9:35   Final debriefing with student leaders.

Preparing for Session Three

1. Work with the leaders of the adult workshop to organize the potluck dinner.

2. Arrange for a panel consisting of a leader from the adult workshop, the adolescent workshop leader, and the host (or others, as appropriate).

3. Things to buy, make copies of, or gather:
    ☐ Milk, apple juice, paper cups, and napkins for refreshments (Student leaders should be bringing brownies.)
    ☐ A copy of the workshop evaluation for each participant.
    ☐ Name tags for everyone, plus markers.
    ☐ Participant registration sheets from Session One.
    ☐ List of assigned small groups and student leaders from Session One.
    ☐ Blank note cards (two or three per participant) and pencils.

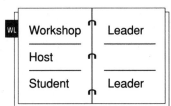

LECTURE OUTLINE: ACCEPTANCE AND HOPE

I. Introduce the third session.

   A. **Ask for feedback.** Thank the participants for returning and ask for comments from Session Two.

   B. **Review.** Ask volunteers to name the first four emotions in the grief cycle (denial, anger, bargaining, depression).

   C. **Preview.** Explain that tonight you'll discuss the last two emotions: acceptance and hope.

II. Discuss acceptance, the fifth emotion in the grief cycle.

   A. **The feeling that we can live with reality** describes acceptance. We are not happy with reality and there has been pain, but we can deal with it. We know we can't change it, and we've stopped trying. We start to work with what is left.

   B. **Student leaders present *The Rhodes Family: Acceptance*.** Discuss how each kid in the family demonstrates acceptance.

III. Discuss hope, the last emotion in the grief cycle.

   A. **Hope is an upbeat, positive feeling.** We begin to see that in the midst of loss, there can be gain. We see some positive things, some options for happiness ahead. After the dark tunnel of grief, we see some light.

   B. **Ask the participants to brainstorm** a list of gains in divorce, such as a better relationship with parents, peace, the end of conflict or even violence, two celebrations of every holiday, new stepparents and siblings, more self-confidence as a result of having more independence and responsibility, and learning about what makes a marriage work or not work.

   C. **Student leaders present *The Rhodes Family: Hope*.** Discuss how long it took each person to reach the stage of hope.

IV. Keeping Out from Between Mom and Dad.

   A. **Explain how parents "triangle" their kids** in their conflict. When the relationship between two parents breaks down, one common way they cope is to ask a third party to convey messages and feelings (such as anger) from one to the other. Parents may use a counselor or lawyer for this, but often they (wrongly) involve their children. (Draw a triangle.) We call this "triangling" the kid in their conflict.

   B. **Parents may use their kids in three ways:**

     1. **As messengers:** "You tell your dad this. . . ."

     2. **As spies or detectives:** "Tell me about your mom's new boyfriend (or furniture)."

     3. **As a dumping ground:** "If you only knew what your dad did to me. . . ."

Workshop	Leader
Host	
Student	Leader

C. **Kids should respectfully step out of the communication** triangle by turning their parents down when they ask them to carry messages. They should especially avoid getting involved in areas such as money, dating, and the grief feelings of their parents. Suggest they say:
- "Mom, please tell Dad that yourself."
- "Dad, I really don't want to answer your questions about Mom's dates."
- "Mom, please stop criticizing Dad. He's still my dad."

D. **Usually parents back off** when they realize what they are doing. Urge the kids to be a friend to their parents, but to stay out of their battles.

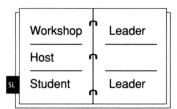

STUDENT LEADERS' OUTLINE OF SESSION ONE

Date of session:

7:20   Adult and student leaders pray together.

7:30   Assigned student leaders greet teen participants as they arrive and help them register.

7:45   Host welcomes group and leads mixer.

   Assigned student leaders divide participants into groups during the mixer.

7:55   Workshop leader offers lectures and student leaders present skits on the first two stages of grief: denial and anger (skits on pp. 97–99).

   Workshop leader conducts a discussion on *Dealing with Mom*.

8:30   Refreshment break.

8:45   Workshop leader leads optional sharing time.

9:00   Student leaders guide *Small-Group Discussion I* (p. 93; begins at 8:45 if sharing time is omitted).

9:25   Closure and invitation to Session Two.

9:30   Adjournment.

9:35   Ten-minute debriefing period with student leaders.

SL

Workshop	Leader
Host	
Student	Leader

STUDENT LEADERS'
OUTLINE OF SESSION TWO

Date of session:

7:20   Adult and student leaders pray together.

7:30   Assigned student leaders greet teen participants as they arrive, register any new people, and assign them to groups.

7:35   Host welcomes group and leads mixer.

7:45   Workshop leader offers lectures and student leaders present skits on the next two stages of grief: bargaining and depression (skits on pp. 100–103).

      Workshop leader conducts a discussion on *Dealing with Dad.*

8:15   Refreshment break.

8:30   Student leaders guide *Small-Group Discussion II* (p. 94).

8:50   Workshop leader and student leaders organize *Family Sculpture.*

9:10   Host moderates an interview with a teen and parent.

9:25   Closure and invitation to Session Three.

9:30   Adjournment.

9:35   Ten-minute debriefing with student leaders.

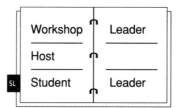

STUDENT LEADERS'
OUTLINE OF SESSION THREE

Date of session:

6:20   Adult and student leaders pray together.

6:30   Student leaders greet teen participants at potluck supper. (Supper includes teens, adults from divorce workshop, and leaders from both workshops. Kids sit together.)

7:10   Adults and students invited to share what their respective workshops have meant to them so far.

7:30   Teens go to their workshop.

7:35   *Family Sculpture* (optional).

7:50   Workshop leader offers lectures and student leaders present skits on the last two stages of grief: acceptance and hope (skits on pp. 104–106).

Workshop leader conducts a discussion on *Keeping Out from Between Mom and Dad.*

8:20   Refreshment break.

8:35   Student leaders guide *Small-Group Discussion III* (p. 95).

9:00   Host moderates panel discussion.

9:25   Participants fill in workshop evaluations.

9:30   Adjournment.

9:35   Final debriefing with student leaders.

Workshop | Leader

Host

Student | Leader

MIXERS

PEOPLE BINGO

Give each person a People-Bingo sheet and a pencil. Explain that they have five minutes to find someone to sign each square on their sheets. No one can sign the same sheet more than twice. At the end of the time limit, have volunteers who completely filled their sheets read the names aloud. If you wish, give the winner a trophy (an old bowling trophy will do) that will stay at your meeting place, "enshrined in that person's honor."

Preparation: Read the categories for *People Bingo* (p. 122) and modify any that are inappropriate for your group. Make copies of the revised sheet for your workshop.

GOOD, CLEAN JOKES

At the second session say something like, "I noticed last week when we did People Bingo that you guys didn't know any really funny *clean* jokes, so I brought some tonight to share with you so you can tell them next time you socialize. They are guaranteed to make you the life of the party."

1. **Why did the man take a pencil to bed?**
   Because he wanted to draw the curtains.
2. **When is the cook mean?**
   When he beats the eggs and whips the cream.
3. **Why was six afraid of seven?**
   Because seven eight (ate) nine.
4. **What's worse than raining cats and dogs?**
   Hailing taxis.
5. **Why was Cinderella a poor football player?**
   Because she had a pumpkin for a coach.
6. **Do you know why Saturday and Sunday are the strongest days?**
   Because the rest are weekdays (weak days).
7. **What dance do Pilgrims do?**
   The Plymouth Rock.
8. **When is it hardest to get a ticket to the moon?**
   When the moon is full.
9. **There were five cats in a boat. One cat jumped out. How many were left?**
   None. They were all copycats.
10. **What do you call a rabbit with a lot of fleas?**
    Bugs Bunny.

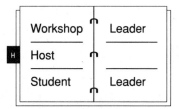

THE SLOGAN GAME

Read the following slogans to the group and ask them to complete the slogan with the product name.

1. The choice of a new generation. *Pepsi*
2. Gentlemen prefer _____ . *Hanes*
3. Oh, what a feeling. *Toyota*
4. We bring good things to life. *General Electric*
5. Where's the beef? *Wendy's*
6. You've come a long way, baby. *Virginia Slims*
7. Tastes great! Less filling! *Bud Lite*
8. Fly the friendly skies. *United Airlines*
9. Can't beat the real thing. *Coke*
10. The unsinkable taste of _____. *Cheerios*
11. I believe in _____, 'cause I believe in me. *Crystal Light*
12. Melts in your mouth, not in your hands. *M&M's*
13. Momma gets it out with _____. *ALL detergent*
14. Just do it! *Nike*
15. It does a body good. *Milk*
16. Reach out and touch someone. *AT&T*
17. Let your fingers do the walking. *Yellow Pages*
18. How do you spell relief? *R-O-L-A-I-D-S*
19. Make a run for the border. *Taco Bell*
20. When you care enough to send the very best. *Hallmark*
21. Don't just go through it, grow through it. *Divorce Recovery Workshop*

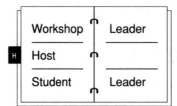

Workshop	Leader
H Host	
Student	Leader

INTERVIEW AND PANEL DISCUSSION

Interview

Ask a teen and parent who are willing to openly discuss their family dynamics to informally speak about their experience with divorce or separation. You may give them prepared questions ahead of time so they can think through their responses, or you may ask spontaneous questions. Allow time for workshop participants to ask questions. The interview enables participants to see the mutual support that is necessary in a single-parent home or a blended family.

Panel Discussion

Distribute blank three-by-five note cards and give participants two minutes to write down any questions they still have concerning divorce or separation. While a student leader collects the cards and sorts them into categories, introduce the panel and invite them to make brief remarks about the workshop. Moderate the discussion by asking the panel questions from the cards and keeping things moving.

Here is a list of typical questions you might use to get things started:

- How do you deal with a parent who has an alcohol problem?
- How do you deal with a parent who wants you to do everything his or her way?
- What should I do when my mom's boyfriend is cold as ice to me?
- I want to talk to my dad, but he has a temper, so I can't say anything. Please tell me how to say what I need to say to him.
- What should you do when you don't like your dad's girlfriend?
- What should I do when I get married so I don't end up getting a divorce?
- Why do my parents argue even after the divorce?
- How should you act when your mom's boyfriend comes to the house?
- How can I help my mom and stepmom be friends—or at least not arch-enemies?
- Do parents who divorce ever get back together?
- Why do you mean by "hope"? Things can't ever be the same.
- Why do we have to put up with parents who try to control us?
- Is it okay for parents to have affairs?

As the question-and-answer period comes to a close, encourage participants to consider seeking God's help in their growth and development. Invite participants who would like counseling—or who just want to talk—to call any of the adult-workshop staff.

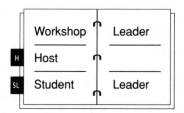

HOW TO BE A BETTER LISTENER

1. **Stop talking!**
   No one can listen and talk at the same time.

2. **Show the listener you want to listen.**
   Stop doodling, making notes, or whatever else you're doing. Look at the speaker without staring. Relax and lean forward. Nod your head and ask questions to show you're interested and want to know more.

3. **Listen to the emotion behind the words.**
   Facial expressions, gestures, tone of voice, and posture all communicate feelings, sometimes more accurately than words. At the same time, don't jump to conclusions. A smile can mean happiness, nervousness, or even contempt. Standing stiffly could indicate fear or uncertainty. Avoiding eye contact can be a sign of lack of interest, anxiety, or (in some cultures) respect. Be aware of these clues and keep an open mind about their meanings.

4. **Listen to understand.**
   Try to see the speaker's point of view, but don't insist you know how the speaker feels. This response from a stranger can turn someone off. Instead, you could mention that your backgrounds are similar in many ways. Keep your own stories to a minimum.

5. **Offer patience, not advice.**
   Listen without interrupting. Some people just need to talk; they don't want advice, just a friendly ear. Be very careful not to offer advice you are not qualified to give.

6. **Don't argue.**
   Most people don't appreciate being told where they are wrong. Just let them express themselves. Then ask a few questions about how they feel or what they think will happen next. Chances are, they will begin to see the issue in a clearer light as a result of describing it to someone else.

7. **Repeat what you think the speaker said.**
   Paraphrase the speaker to make sure you understand and to help him or her think about the problem.

8. **Respect the speaker's privacy.**
   Don't try to force someone to share feelings. Instead, provide a friendly, relaxed situation where the listener will feel free to talk. Let your relationship develop naturally.

9. **Stop talking!**
   Some people think we have two ears and one mouth because God meant us to listen twice as much as we talk.

HOW TO LEAD A SMALL GROUP

1. **Start with ground rules.**
   Here are three that will help everyone feel comfortable:
   - You don't have to talk if you don't want to.
   - Everything said here is confidential. None of it is to be repeated to *anyone* outside the group.
   - This is *our* group. We all share responsibility for its success.

2. **Avoid dominating discussions.**
   Nothing will turn people off faster than a group leader who won't let anyone else talk. Your role is to draw members into the discussion, keep things on track, and put people at ease. Instead of providing answers, you need to help group members find their own answers. If something comes up that does need a specific response, ask the workshop leader or another adult leader to help.

3. **Make sure everyone has an opportunity to talk.**
   If someone is dominating the discussion, break in tactfully and ask other group members what they think about the same subject. Ask specific members to comment instead of asking, "Does anyone else have anything to say?"

   On the other hand, if someone seems hap-pier just listening, don't force that person to participate. Given time, most teenagers will want to take part in the discussions.

4. **Ask open-ended, nonjudgmental questions.**
   The way you ask questions can help group members to either relax and enter into the discussion or to put up their guards. Avoid questions that put people on the spot, that ask them to make a judgment, or that can be answered simply "yes" or "no":
   - Instead of asking, "Do you feel depressed sometimes?" ask, "What is something that can make kids feel depressed after their parents divorce?"
   - Instead of, "What's wrong with blended families?" ask, "How do you feel about blended families?"
   - Instead of, "Should parents date?" ask, "What are some things that happen when parents start dating?"

5. **When time is up, don't be afraid to quit.**
   You don't have to discuss every question on the list. It's actually a good idea to stop the discussion when people are really into it. If they want to talk more about some issue, encourage them to come to the next session.

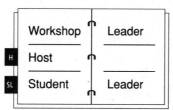

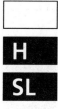

SMALL-GROUP DISCUSSION QUESTIONS I

1. Begin by introducing yourself and telling a little about your own family and the reasons you volunteered to help with the workshop. Then explain these ground rules:
   - You don't have to talk if you don't want to.
   - Everything said here is confidential. None of it is to be repeated to *anyone* outside the group.
   - This is *our* group. We all share responsibility for its success.

2. When everyone is feeling comfortable, ask participants to
   - Tell where they live and go to school.
   - Describe their families and whom they live with.
   - Name things they like to do.
   - Tell how long ago their parents separated or divorced.
   - For volunteers only: Why do you think your parents split up?

3. Point out that tonight the group discussed denial and anger. Ask the following questions:
   - Did anything happen recently that you tried to pretend didn't happen? What was it?
   - Is anyone in your family denying the reality of your parents' divorce?
   - Did you get really angry recently? What was the problem?
   - How do you express anger?
   - What are some positive ways we can express anger in our families?

Workshop | Leader
H Host
SL Student | Leader

SMALL-GROUP DISCUSSION QUESTIONS II

1. To refresh everyone's memories, ask participants to tell the group their names and where they live. Remind the group of the ground rules:
   - You don't have to talk if you don't want to.
   - Everything said here is confidential. None of it is to be repeated to *anyone* outside the group.
   - This is *our* group. We all share responsibility for its success.
2. Ask volunteers to share one idea they remember from last week's workshop.
3. Ask the group what changes they have seen in their parents during or since the divorce/separation. What changes have they seen in themselves?

4. Point out that tonight we talked about bargaining. Ask the following questions:
   - Has anyone tried to bargain for something recently with their parent or parents?
   - Did it have anything to do with the divorce? What happened?
5. We also talked about how it's normal to feel depressed when your parents divorce. Ask the following questions:
   - Has anyone felt depressed recently?
   - How did you show it?
   - What are some things we can do when we're feeling depressed?

Mention that, while adults and some young people may withdraw during depression, many kids act angry when they are depressed in an attempt to deal with their feelings. They may even try antisocial things like shoplifting, getting drunk, or driving recklessly.

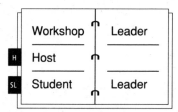

SMALL-GROUP DISCUSSION QUESTIONS III

1. Open the discussion by asking volunteers to describe a happy time with their families.

2. Encourage participants to share any problems they're facing with either parent.
   - Are anyone's parents dating? What's that like?
   - Does anyone have a new stepmom or stepdad? Any problems there?
   - How about stepbrothers or sisters?

3. Point out that tonight the workshop leader talked about parents "using" kids. Ask the following questions:
   - Has either of your parents ever tried to use you as a messenger, an informant, or a dumping ground for complaints?
   - How did it make you feel?
   - What are some ways we can get out from between our parents and their conflicts?

4. Tonight we discussed acceptance. Ask the following questions:
   - How are you doing in accepting your parents' divorce?
   - Are there still some things that are hard to accept? How can we help?

5. We also discussed hope. Ask the following questions:
   - What hopes do you have for your own future (such as a fun vacation, college, dating, a happier family)?
   - Is it easy or hard for you to have hope right now? Why?

Workshop	Leader
Host	
Student	Leader

SAMPLE LETTER FROM STUDENT LEADERS TO PARTICIPANTS

Dear_____,

    I just wanted to drop you a quick note to thank you for coming to our group on (Tuesday, Wednesday, etc.) night. You really helped with your (smile, sense of humor, comments, etc.).

    I hope at the next session I can get to know you a little better. I look forward to seeing you there!

Sincerely,

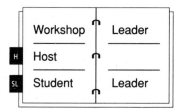

THE RHODES FAMILY: DENIAL

SET: *The living room in the Rhodes' home. DAD and ERIC are seated. ROBBIE is wherever he can be set up. MOM and SUSAN say their introductory lines to the audience while standing beside their seats onstage. Then they sit down to join the action.*

MOM: The Rhodes family has three children: Susan, fourteen; Eric, ten; and Robbie, six. Susan tells the first part of the story.

SUSAN: One evening Mom and Dad called us into the living room for a family meeting. They called these meetings every so often to discuss household responsibilities. Once my brothers and I called a family meeting to vote on a raise in our allowances, but we lost. Dad said he had the right to veto. Tonight Dad started the meeting.

DAD: Well kids, your mother and I have something to discuss with you.

ERIC: (*interrupting*) I hope you're not going to make me start mowing the lawn!

MOM shoots ERIC a look that says, "This meeting is more serious than usual."

DAD: (*clearing his throat*) You all realize that people change as they grow older. Susan's gotten taller and likes rock music now. Eric likes some vegetables he used to hate, and Robbie, who used to hate being alone at night, wants his own room.

Everyone freezes except SUSAN, who partially stands and speaks as an aside to the audience.

SUSAN: I don't know where this is heading, but my nervous stomach tells me we aren't here to discuss building a room onto the house for Robbie.

Everyone resumes action.

DAD: In much the same way, your mother and I have changed. We argue more than we used to and we don't like the same things we used to like.

ERIC: (*interrupting again*) No, you don't! I never hear you argue!

MOM looks at ERIC sadly.

DAD: Your mother and I have decided it will be best if she and I live apart for a while.

Everyone freezes as SUSAN stands straight up indignantly, speaking to the audience.

SUSAN: I can't believe what I'm hearing. I don't think they argue that much either. (*sits and speaks to MOM*) How long is "a while"?

MOM: It's hard to say. We'll probably talk it over in a month to see how

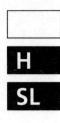

things are going. Right now we just feel it would be best to spend some time apart.

ROBBIE: Am I going with you, Dad?

DAD: No. You're all going to stay here with your mom. I'm going to rent an apartment near my office.

ROBBIE: I'm going out to play now. See you later, Dad. (*makes running action with the "legs" and ducks behind the sheet*)

MOM: (*sighing*) Well, I've got supper to make. (*exits*)

DAD: I guess I better pack. (*exits*)

ERIC: (*sitting on the couch with his head in his hand*) I know this is all my fault. They always fight when I get in trouble at school.

SUSAN: (*patting his shoulder*) No, Eric. It didn't have anything to do with you. I don't know whose fault it is. (*pausing*) I wonder if I should tell my friends.

Adapted from Excerpts from Stages Curriculum, Guidance Resources, Irvine Unified School District, 5050 Barranca, Irvine, CA 92714.

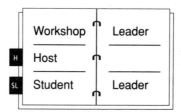

THE RHODES FAMILY: ANGER

SET: SUSAN, ERIC, *and* ROBBIE *are around the breakfast table. There's a telephone near the table.* MOM *introduces the skit at center-front stage and then joins the action.*

MOM: (*to the audience*) It's been six months since Matt moved out. The separation has become a divorce, but the word *divorce* still scares me. Like millions of other couples, we never thought we would get divorced. In the end, we felt it was best for us, but we were concerned about how the kids would take it. The morning I told the kids we had to sell the house and move, Susan exploded at the breakfast table.

SUSAN: (*shouting*) We can't move! We've always lived in this house. This is all your fault! First you make Dad move out and now you want me to move away from all my friends! I think you're a terrible mother. I'll go live with my friends if we move! (*runs offstage*)

MOM: (*stares at the door, ready to cry. Speaks to the closed door*) I'm angry, too. What have I done wrong? This wasn't what I expected my life to be like.

Walks to the table and sees that ROBBIE *and* ERIC *aren't eating their breakfasts anymore.*

ROBBIE: (*hugs* MOM) I love you, Mommy.

MOM: (*looks at* ERIC, *who's staring into his lap*) You better go or you'll be late for school. (*boys exit*)

Phone rings.

MOM: Hello? (*pause*) Yes, this is Marie Rhodes. (*pause*) You have someone who wants to look at the house? (*dejectedly*) Oh. I mean, great. Bring them over. (*hangs up and looks around the kitchen*) I can't stand the idea of someone else living here.

Phone rings again.

MOM: Hello? (*pause*) Oh, Mrs. Fields. (*pause*) Eric was in a fight this morning? (*pause*) I know this is not the first time. I'm glad you called to—(*pause*) And he hasn't done his homework? But he did it. I helped him. (*pause*) Yes, well I'll speak to him. (*pause*) Thank you. Goodbye. (*starting to clear the table*) "Bad news comes in threes." I'm glad that's just superstition.

Phone rings again.

MOM: Oh, no! Hello? (*pause*) The school nurse? (*pause*) Which school? I mean, whose school? (*pause*) Robbie's sick? (*pause*) A bad stomachache. Yes, I'll be right over to pick him up. (*hangs up with a sigh and exits*)

Adapted from Excerpts from Stages Curriculum, Guidance Resources, Irvine Unified School District, 5050 Barranca, Irvine, CA 92714.

THE RHODES FAMILY: BARGAINING

SET: *In the kitchen MOM is fixing dinner and ERIC is facing the audience near the stage entrance.*

MOM: Eric, now age eleven, tells the Rhodes family story, one year after the divorce.

ERIC: When our parents first got divorced, Dad didn't even seem like our dad. When we went to stay with him every other weekend, he always acted like it was somebody's birthday. He took us to the zoo, an amusement park, the movies, everywhere! It was kind of fun at first, but this past weekend, Robbie, Susan, and I just wanted to watch cartoons. I think Dad was glad we didn't want to go anywhere. Anyway, Dad drove us back home Sunday night. When we got there, Susan asked Dad if he would help us carry in our stuff. And Dad did. Then he started talking to Mom.

ROBBIE: Are you staying for dinner, Dad?

MOM and DAD look at each other dubiously.

MOM: There's more than enough, Matt. You're welcome to stay if you'll set the table.

ERIC: (*runs offstage shouting*) Susan! Dad's staying for dinner!

SUSAN: (*shouting from offstage*) So? Big deal.

All freeze.

ERIC: (*entering, talking to audience*) Boy, something weird must happen to you when you turn fifteen! I can never tell what Susan is going to like anymore. (*shrugs*) Dinner was fine, but nobody talked very much. When they did, they were really nice to each other. I even said please when I asked Robbie to pass the milk.

Thaw, and DAD exits while ROBBIE, ERIC, and SUSAN lie down as if going to bed.

ERIC: Dad left after dinner. Susan, Robbie, and I had to finish our homework, pack our lunches for the next day, and get ready for bed. Mom came around to say good night to us. I heard her talking to Susan first.

SUSAN: Mom, if I do all my chores next Saturday morning, can I spend the night at Amy's house?

MOM: Sure, as long as you do your chores first.

SUSAN: (*after a pause*) It was nice having Dad here for dinner tonight, Mom. Maybe he'll cook dinner for you now, to pay you back.

MOM laughs quietly as she walks to ROBBIE.

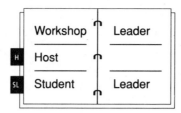

ERIC: (*up on his elbow, talking to audience*) Maybe Mom and Dad got into fights because of me. That worries me. Maybe if I promise never to get into trouble at school again, they'll get married again.

ROBBIE: Mom, do you think you and Dad will always be divorced, even when I'm grown up?

ERIC: (*sitting up suddenly and looking at the audience*) Oh brother! Robbie's questions always surprise me. He asks things I'm afraid to ask. (*plops back down on his bed*)

MOM: (*sighing*) I guess we'll always be divorced, Robbie. One of us could get married to someone else, though.

ERIC: (*rolling over on one elbow to talk to audience*) I've never thought about either one of them getting married again. Now I've really got to get them back together before that happens.

MOM *leaves* ROBBIE *to come to* ERIC.

ERIC: Oh boy, here comes Mom. I'm going to pretend I'm asleep. If I start talking I might start crying, too.

Adapted from Excerpts from Stages Curriculum, Guidance Resources, Irvine Unified School District, 5050 Barranca, Irvine, CA 92714.

THE RHODES FAMILY: DEPRESSION

SET: *The kitchen at* DAD*'s apartment.* ERIC, SUSAN, *and* ROBBIE *are sitting around the table with* DAD.

MOM: (*center-front stage, to audience*) This part of the story is told by Mr. Rhodes a year and a half after the divorce. (*exits*)

DAD: (*standing beside the table, to audience*) I looked forward to having the kids for the long holiday weekend. It seemed as if I hadn't seen them in months, but it had only been two weeks. I calculated that in the last year and a half, I had seen the kids about eighty-four days, less than three months. I thought about trying to get joint custody, but Marie and I lived so far apart that it hardly seemed practical—or fair to the children. Sometimes I'd work late, something I found myself doing a lot, and go home to an empty apartment. I'd walk through the rooms looking for someone who needed help on their homework or needed to be tucked into bed. When the kids arrived Friday evening, I had dinner almost ready and a busy schedule of activities planned for the next three days. It started with a movie that night. But when I told the kids about it, I got mixed reactions.

SUSAN: I'll pass. I already saw that one.

ROBBIE: I'll go if you really want to, Dad.

ERIC: (*pause*) Couldn't we just stay here tonight, Dad? I don't really feel much like going anywhere.

DAD: (*to audience*) So much for Plan A. (*to kids, again*) Sure. That's fine with me. (*pause*) By the way, Susan, how's school going?

Kids freeze, DAD *speaks to audience.*

DAD: Susan had planned on going to Newmark High School since she was eight. She had memorized Newmark's football cheers by age ten. By the time she was twelve, she had mapped out her courses for all four years at Newmark. When Marie sold the house and moved, Susan had to leave her friends and go to Newmark's rival high school across town. It was a hard adjustment.

Thaw. ERIC *starts shuffling from one side of the stage to another, picking up a prop—like a Rubic's Cube, Slinky, paperweight—and putting it down without interest.*

SUSAN: (*sighing*) School's all right, I suppose. But the teachers aren't as good as the ones at Newmark and the football team is horrible.

DAD: (*watching* ERIC) Well, Honey, teams can get better. (*to* ERIC *and trying to sound cheerful*) Do you have any homework you need help with?

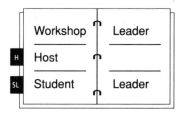

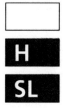

ERIC: (*distractedly*) Huh? Oh. No, the teacher didn't give any. I guess she figured nobody would have time. A lot of people were going away for the weekend.

DAD: Where were they going?

ERIC: All the scouts are off on a camping trip. (*stops his restless pacing and stares at the floor*)

DAD: Your troop? (ERIC *nods*) Didn't you want to go?

ERIC: (*mumbling*) Well, kind of. But this was my weekend to be with you.

DAD: What?

ERIC: (*looking up miserably at* DAD) I said, this was my weekend to be with you.

DAD: Look, Eric, if you have something special you want to do on a weekend, just call and tell me.

ERIC: I wanted to come here, too, Dad. I wanted to do both things. (*freeze*)

DAD: (*to audience*) I can imagine Eric trying all week to decide what he wanted to do. Did he want to go with his friends or come here and be with me? Probably in the end he just went along with what had already been planned. I want him to do things that are important to him (*taking a deep breath and blowing it out again*), even if it means I see him less. (*thaw*) Eric, if you miss a weekend with me, I'm sure your mom will let you come another weekend by yourself.

ERIC: (*looking happy*) Really? That's a great idea! Thanks!

ERIC *and* SUSAN *exit.*

DAD: (*to audience*) The next day we were going to ride our bikes to the park and have a picnic. As we got ready to leave, Robbie came running up.

ROBBIE: (*shouting*) Dad! My bike is missing! I can't find it anywhere! (*biting his lower lip to hold back his tears*)

DAD: (*shoulders sagging*) Oh, Robbie. Didn't you put it inside the patio fence?

ROBBIE *shakes his head, turns, and slowly shuffles offstage.* DAD *speaks to audience.*

DAD: We searched, to no avail. The bike was gone. Poor Robbie spent the rest of the weekend like a lost puppy, crying about his bike. Monday night after the kids were gone, I glanced at the schedule of activities I had planned for the weekend. We'd done nothing on the list.

Adapted from Excerpts from Stages Curriculum, Guidance Resources, Irvine Unified School District, 5050 Barranca, Irvine, CA 92714.

THE RHODES FAMILY: ACCEPTANCE

SET: *In the kitchen of* MOM's *home. Drop the "Little Nemo" gig for* ROBBIE *for these last two skits.*

DAD: Robbie, now age eight, tells this episode of the Rhodes family's story.

ROBBIE: (*stage front, to audience*) I pedaled my bike around the corner and tried to catch up to the blue car in front of me.   It was Mr. Lesser's car. He was on his way to see my mom. He's sort of a nice man, I guess. At first, I didn't like him at all, but at first, I didn't like any of Mom's dates—I even spit on one man. That was when I was a lot younger. Mr. Lesser is better than the rest. One time he took Eric and me to a baseball game, and we had fun. Anyway, I got off my bike and ran into the house just as he was saying "Hi" to Mom. (*to* MR. LESSER) Are you and my mom going out tonight?

LESSER: As a matter of fact, Robbie, I'm fixing dinner for all of you tonight. Want to give me a hand with the groceries?

ROBBIE: You're fixing dinner? I can't believe it. My dad never fixed dinner when he lived with us. Of course, he does now 'cause he lives alone. (*thoughtfully to audience*) Maybe it is okay for men to cook after all. (*to* LESSER *as they unload the groceries and* MOM *starts toward the exit*) Mom's probably gonna change out of her work clothes. She's a secretary for some lawyers. She didn't want to be a secretary at first. She thought she could get paid more for something besides typing. Now she seems to like her job a little better, but she still doesn't make much money.

SUSAN: (*intercepting* MOM *near exit*) Mom, I paid for my car insurance, so can I drive the car to work tonight?

MOM: Sure, Honey. That was our agreement.

SUSAN: Thanks, Mom, you're great.

MOM *puts her arm around* SUSAN *and they exit.*

ROBBIE: (*still talking to* LESSER, *who nods and "hmms" but can't get a word in*) A few weeks ago, Susan was really mad at Mom. Mom told her that if she wanted to drive the car, she would have to pay for her own insurance. Of course, Susan tried to get her own way. First, she yelled at Mom. Then she called Dad and cried. I guess her crying didn't work, because the next day she got a job at the movie theater selling popcorn. She's *sooooo* lucky! She sees every movie as many times as she wants and gets free soda and popcorn!

ERIC *enters, looking for a pencil.*

ROBBIE: When I'm old enough, that's where I'm going to work! (*leaves* LESSER *to pull on* ERIC's *sleeve*) Hey, Eric. Guess what! Mr. Lesser is fixing

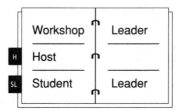

dinner for us tonight!

ERIC: I know, Robbie. Mom told me earlier.

ROBBIE: Want to help me practice batting?

ERIC: Nah, I want to finish all of my homework tonight so I can play all weekend. I'll help you tomorrow before your game.

ROBBIE: You sure study a lot! Ever since Mom and Dad talked to your counselor at school, that's all you do.

ERIC: Well, junior high is harder than grade school, you know. Besides, if I want to keep playing sports, I have to bring my grades up. (*exits*)

ROBBIE: (*to* LESSER, *who's starting to cook dinner*) Maybe I'll go upstairs with Eric (*pauses, considering*) Nah, it's not too exciting watching Eric study. You need any help with dinner?

LESSER: I think I could use the help of another man.

Adapted from Excerpts from Stages Curriculum, Guidance Resources, Irvine Unified School District, 5050 Barranca, Irvine, CA 92714.

THE RHODES FAMILY: HOPE

MOM: It's two and a half years since our divorce. Who would have ever thought I'd be going to college at the same time as my daughter? I didn't think I'd be working either, but now I'm doing both! I've been a receptionist in a law office since last year. I enjoy the work, but the money is hardly enough to buy the food we need. So this year I enrolled in classes at the junior college to become a legal secretary. Some days I wish I could go back to the way things were three years ago, but most days I enjoy my work and get excited about becoming a legal secretary.

SUSAN: At first I felt like Mom and Dad's divorce ruined my life. I hated my new school and I didn't know anybody. But once I got used to my new school, I really started to like it. I made a lot of new friends and was on the school newspaper staff. I never would have done that at Newmark. There only the honors kids were on the newspaper staff. It set me up to major in journalism now at the junior college. Sometimes, though, when I talk to my old friends, I wish Mom and Dad were still together and we still lived in our old house. But since they both seem happier now, I guess it was all for the best.

ROBBIE: Last weekend I had a soccer game, and I scored two goals. My mom and dad were both at the game, and afterwards they took me out for a "pig-out"—twelve scoops of ice cream! It was neat! It was almost as though we were still a family, except when Dad lived with us, he was always too busy to watch Eric or me play in any games. Now he comes to all my games! And when we go to see him on weekends, he's a lot of fun. We don't always go someplace, but we always have a good time.

ERIC: Starting junior high was the pits. My mom was always on my case about my grades. I just didn't like school, and it seemed like none of the kids liked me. Mom was always too busy to talk to me. Finally, Mom and Dad talked together. Afterward they asked me if I'd like to live with Dad. At first I thought they meant Dad was going to live with us again—what wishful thinking! So next month I move in with Dad. Then I'll visit Mom every other weekend. I know I'll miss Mom, but I think I'll like living with Dad. Mom seems to think it will be a good experience for me.

DAD: I'm looking forward to having Eric move in with me. Sometimes, though, I wonder if Marie and I could have done something earlier to prevent our divorce. I know it was hard on the kids—on us, too. But there's no point in thinking about the past. Besides, we're both much happier at this point and we're still good friends.

Adapted from Excerpts from Stages Curriculum, Guidance Resources, Irvine Unified School District, 5050 Barranca, Irvine, CA 92714.

APPENDIX A
WORKSHOP FORMS AND LETTERS

LOGOS

ADVANCE REGISTRATION SHEET
For the Adolescent Divorce Recovery Workshop

Parents: If you plan to send one or more of your children to the Adolescent Divorce Recovery Workshop, please place a check mark in the appropriate column below to tell us your child's sex and grade level. That way we can plan ahead. The workshop dates are as follows:

Grade Levels

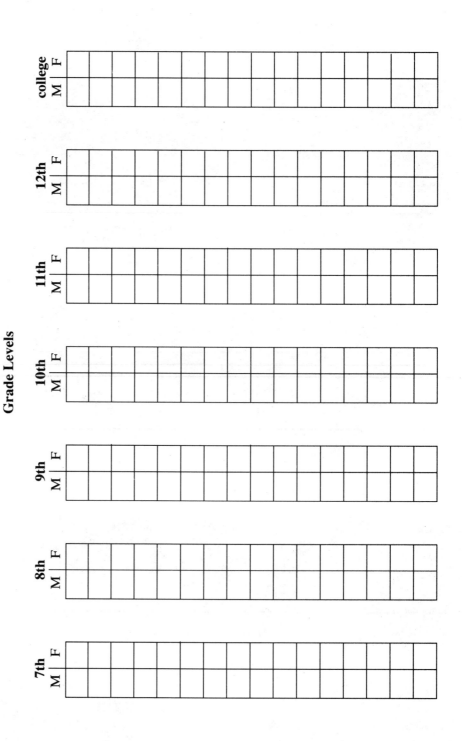

REGISTRATION SHEET
High School Girls

Name	Street Address	City	Zip	Phone	School/Grade
1.					
2.					
3.					
4.					
5.					
6.					
7.					
8.					
9.					
10.					
11.					
12.					
13.					
14.					
15.					
16.					

REGISTRATION SHEET
High School Boys

Name	Street Address	City	Zip	Phone	School/Grade
1.					
2.					
3.					
4.					
5.					
6.					
7.					
8.					
9.					
10.					
11.					
12.					
13.					
14.					
15.					
16.					

REGISTRATION SHEET
Junior High Girls

Name	Street Address	City	Zip	Phone	School/Grade
1.					
2.					
3.					
4.					
5.					
6.					
7.					
8.					
9.					
10.					
11.					
12.					
13.					
14.					
15.					
16.					

REGISTRATION SHEET
Junior High Boys

Name	Street Address	City	Zip	Phone	School/Grade
1.					
2.					
3.					
4.					
5.					
6.					
7.					
8.					
9.					
10.					
11.					
12.					
13.					
14.					
15.					
16.					

ADOLESCENT DIVORCE RECOVERY
WORKSHOP EVALUATION

I felt the workshop was

☐ extremely helpful
☐ somewhat helpful
☐ not too helpful

What did you like most? ————————————————————

————————————————————————————————————

————————————————————————————————————

What did you like least? ————————————————————

————————————————————————————————————

————————————————————————————————————

Any suggestions for the next workshop? ——————————

————————————————————————————————————

————————————————————————————————————

————————————————————————————————————

————————————————————————————————————

ADOLESCENT DIVORCE RECOVERY
WORKSHOP EVALUATION

I felt the workshop was

☐ extremely helpful
☐ somewhat helpful
☐ not too helpful

What did you like most? ————————————————————

————————————————————————————————————

————————————————————————————————————

What did you like least? ————————————————————

————————————————————————————————————

————————————————————————————————————

Any suggestions for the next workshop? ——————————

————————————————————————————————————

————————————————————————————————————

————————————————————————————————————

————————————————————————————————————

SAMPLE RECRUITMENT LETTER
TO SEND TO POTENTIAL STUDENT LEADERS

Dear _____,

We are beginning to put together our student leadership team for our Adolescent Divorce Recovery Workshop, and we invite you to apply. The workshop helps young people cope with the separation or divorce of their parents. It has three sessions, meeting (*dates*) at (*place*) from (*time to time*). (*Student leaders come a little earlier and stay a few minutes later.*)

Student leaders help at the workshop by greeting and registering participants, leading small-group discussions, and generally making the young people who attend feel welcome and comfortable. (You'll also be asked to bake brownies—from a mix—for refreshments!)

To help prepare the leaders we select, we have scheduled a leader dinner and training session on (*date*) at (*place*) from (*time to time*). At this session we'll get acquainted, describe the student leader's role, make assignments, and go over the format of the three sessions.

If this sounds like something you'd enjoy—and if you can attend the training and ALL THREE workshop sessions—please fill out the application form I've enclosed and return it to me by (*deadline*).

I look forward to hearing from you! If you have any questions or concerns, please call me at (*phone number*).

Sincerely,

APPLICATION FOR NEW STUDENT LEADERS
ADOLESCENT DIVORCE RECOVERY
WORKSHOP

Your name _____

Parent(s) name(s) _____

Address _____

Phone _____

School/Grade _____

Church _____

Please answer the following questions briefly:

1. Are your parents ☐ separated ☐ divorced ☐ remarried?

2. Have you ever participated in a Divorce Recovery Workshop? ☐ yes ☐ no

   If yes, when, where, and who were the leaders? _____

   _____

3. Have you ever led a small group? ☐ yes ☐ no
   If yes, where and what kind? How would you describe the experience?_____

   _____

   _____

4. What does your Christian faith mean to you? _____

   _____

   _____

5. Do you recall a specific time when God became real to you? Please explain _____

   _____

   _____

   _____

SAMPLE LEADER-IN-TRAINING RECRUITMENT LETTER TO SEND TO FORMER WORKSHOP PARTICIPANTS

Dear _____,

We are beginning to select student leaders for our next Adolescent Divorce Recovery Workshop and would like to know if you are interested. Because you attended one of our previous workshops, we feel you have the background and skills to be an asset to our workshop program.

We try to select at least half of our student leaders from those who have already helped lead workshops for us. The remaining leaders-in-training are people like you, who have been participants at a workshop.

This workshop is scheduled on (*dates*) from (*time to time*) at (*place*). We'll begin with a leader dinner and training session on (*date*) from (*time to time*) at (*place*). If this sounds interesting to you and you can attend ALL THREE workshop sessions and the leader-training dinner, please call me at (*phone number*) as soon as possible to schedule an informal interview.

If you have any questions or concerns, call me at (*phone number*). We look forward to including you on our student leadership team!

Sincerely,

SAMPLE RECRUITMENT LETTER
TO SEND TO FORMER STUDENT LEADERS

Dear _____,

   Our next Adolescent Divorce Recovery Workshop will be held (*dates, times, place*). Can we count on you to help us again?

   We really appreciate all your efforts and support in past workshops and look forward to working with you again. Your commitment to this ministry is very special.

   I'm enclosing a stamped postcard for your reply. Please return it as soon as possible to let us know if you can be on our student leadership team one more time.

                              Sincerely,

SAMPLE LETTER
CONFIRMING LEADERS' SELECTION

Dear _____,

Welcome to our student leadership team!

We look forward to working with you and want to make sure you have the dates for the leader dinner and training session and all three workshop sessions on your calendar. Here they are:

(*dates, times, locations of training + three sessions*)

At the training session we'll all get better acquainted, and you'll find out what to expect at each workshop session. We'll also make specific assignments, answer all your questions, and visit the adult divorce workshop together to encourage the adults attending to send their kids to our sessions.

We value your commitment to this ministry and feel we have a special group of student leaders and leaders-in-training. If you have any questions before the training session, please call me. If your plans change, be certain to let me know right away so we can to make any adjustments in our plans.

See you (*date of training session*)!

Sincerely,

SAMPLE THANK-YOU LETTER

Dear _____,

Thank you for your time and efforts during the recent Adolescent Divorce Recovery Workshop. We appreciate all you did to help other young people through a difficult time in their lives. As you know, caring people like yourself make this time a little easier.

I hope you will be willing to help us on another workshop. I'll be in touch with you as soon as we have one scheduled! Thanks again for your help!

Sincerely,

PEOPLE BINGO

Instructions: Find someone to sign each square on this sheet. The same person can sign only two squares. You can sign only one yourself!

A GUY WHO IS 17	A BOY WITH BLONDE HAIR	A SENIOR IN HIGH SCHOOL	SOMEONE WHO CAN TELL A *FUNNY* JOKE
AN ATHLETE WHO IS IN TRAINING NOW	A MUSICIAN	SOMEONE WITH BRACES	SOMEONE WITH AN EARRING
SOMEONE WHO MOVED HERE LESS THAN THREE MONTHS AGO	SOMEONE WHO WATCHES SOAP OPERAS	A GIRL WITH A DRIVER'S LICENSE	SOMEONE WHO HAS BEEN TO HAWAII
SOMEONE BORN IN ANOTHER COUNTRY	SOMEONE WHO LOVES TO EAT LIVER	A GIRL WHO IS 13	SOMEONE IN JUNIOR HIGH OR MIDDLE SCHOOL

APPENDIX B
ONE-DAY WORKSHOP

Doing the divorce recovery workshop as a one-day seminar may suit your kids' needs better or may allow you to bring in an especially qualified workshop leader who could not otherwise lead for you. Use the information and reproducible pages from the basic workshop to prepare for the one-day workshop: premise and goals, adolescent needs, time line, staff, budget and publicity, physical arrangement, and refreshments.

Train the student leaders as for the basic workshop, offering them the same handouts—except for substituting the outline of the all-day session, the alternate discussion questions, and the alternative follow-up letter, all found in Appendix B. Assign student leaders the same duties for greeting, brownies (for afternoon break), discussion-leading teams, registering, and breaking the participants into small groups. Assign a couple of student leaders to bring cut-up fruit for the morning break.

Overview

The all-day workshop is divided into five forty-minute sessions interspersed with mixers, group discussions, skits and an interview. It runs from 8:30 a.m. to 4:30 p.m. (including breaks and lunch).

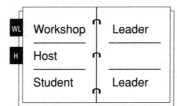

OUTLINE OF ONE-DAY WORKSHOP

Overview

Date of session:

8:20   Adult and student leaders pray together.

8:30   Assigned student leaders greet teen participants as they arrive and help them register.

8:45   Host welcomes group and leads *People Bingo* (p. 88 and 122).
Assigned student leaders divide participants into groups during the mixer (see p. 75, "Dividing Participants into Groups").

9:00   Workshop leader offers lectures and student leaders present skits on the first two stages of grief: denial and anger (lecture outline begins on p. 76).

9:45   Student leaders guide *Small-Group Discussion IV.*

10:25   Refreshment break.

10:45   Workshop leader conducts a discussion on *Dealing with Mom* (discussion outline on p. 77).

11:00   Workshop leader offers lectures and student leaders present skits on the next two stages of grief: bargaining and depression (lecture outline begins on p. 80).

11:40   Workshop leader and student leaders organize *Family Sculpture* (p. 81).

11:50   Ten-minute debriefing with student leaders.

12:00   Lunch break.

1:00   Host moderates an interview with a teen and parent (p. 90).

1:20   Workshop leader leads a discussion on *Dealing with Dad* (discussion outline on p. 80).

1:35   Workshop leader offers lectures and student leaders present skits on the last two stages of grief: acceptance and hope (lecture outline begins on p. 83).

2:05   Student leaders guide *Small-Group Discussion V.*
Student leaders hand out 3 x 5 cards and pencils for participants to write out questions for the upcoming panel discussion.

2:45   Refreshment break.

3:00   Workshop leader conducts discussion on *Keeping Out from Between Mom and Dad* (discussion outline on p. 83).

3:15   Host moderates panel discussion (p. 90).

3:45   *Family Sculpture* (optional).

4:00   Workshop leader leads optional sharing time (p. 77).

4:20   Participants fill in workshop evaluations (Appendix A).

4:30   Adjournment.

4:35   Final debriefing with student leaders (p. 78).

```
┌──────────────────────────┐
│ Workshop  ⌐  Leader       │
│ ─────────    ─────────    │
│ Host      ⌐               │
│ ─────────    ─────────    │
│ SL Student ⌐ Leader       │
└──────────────────────────┘
```

STUDENT LEADERS'
OUTLINE OF ONE-DAY WORKSHOP

Date of session:

8:20   Adult and student leaders pray together.

8:30   Assigned student leaders greet teen participants as they arrive and help them register.

8:45   Host welcomes group and leads mixer.

      Assigned student leaders divide participants into groups during the mixer.

9:00   Workshop leader offers lectures and student leaders present skits on the first two stages of grief: denial and anger (skits on pp. 97–99).

9:45   Student leaders guide *Small-Group Discussion IV* (p. 127).

10:25 Refreshment break.

10:45 Workshop leader conducts a discussion on *Dealing with Mom*.

11:00 Workshop leader offers lectures and student leaders present skits on the next two stages of grief: bargaining and depression (skits on pp. 100—103).

11:40 Workshop leader and student leaders organize *Family Sculpture*.

11:50 Ten-minute debriefing with student leaders.

12:00 Lunch break.

1:00   Host moderates an interview with a teen and parent.

1:20   Workshop leader conducts a discussion on *Dealing with Dad*.

1:35   Workshop leader offers lectures and student leaders present skits on the last two stages of grief: acceptance and hope (skits on pp. 104–106).

2:05   Student leaders guide *Small-Group Discussion V* (p. 128).

      Student leaders hand out 3 x 5 cards and pencils for participants to write out questions for the upcoming panel discussion.

2:45   Refreshment break.

3:00   Workshop leader conducts discussion on *Keeping Out from Between Mom and Dad*.

3:15   Host moderates panel discussion.

3:45   *Family Sculpture* (optional).

4:00   Workshop leader leads optional sharing time.

4:20   Participants fill in workshop evaluations.

4:30   Adjournment.

4:35   Final debriefing with student leaders.

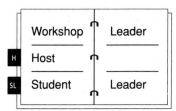

SMALL-GROUP DISCUSSION IV

1. Begin by introducing yourself and telling a little about your own family and the reasons you volunteered to help with the workshop. Then explain these ground rules:
   - You don't have to talk if you don't want to.
   - Everything said here is confidential. None of it is to be repeated to *anyone* outside the group.
   - This is *our* group. We all share responsibility for its success.

2. When everyone is feeling comfortable, ask participants to
   - Give their names.
   - Tell where they live and go to school.
   - Describe their families and whom they live with.
   - Name things they like to do.
   - Tell how long ago their parents separated or divorced.
   - For volunteers only: Why do you think your parents split up?

3. Point out that this morning the group discussed denial and anger. Ask the following questions:
   - Did anything happen recently that you tried to pretend didn't happen? What was it?
   - Is anyone in your family denying the reality of your parents' divorce?
   - Did you get really angry recently? What was the problem?
   - How do you express anger?
   - What are some positive ways we can express anger in our families?

Workshop | Leader

H Host |

SL Student | Leader

SMALL-GROUP DISCUSSION V

1. Ask volunteers to share one idea that was new to them from the workshop so far.

2. Ask the group what changes they have seen in their parents during or since the divorce/separation. What changes have they seen in themselves?

3. Point out that today we talked about bargaining. Ask:
   • Has anyone tried to bargain for something recently with their parent or parents?
   • Did it have anything to do with the divorce? What happened?

4. We also talked about how it's normal to feel depressed when your parents divorce. Ask the following questions:
   • Has anyone felt depressed recently?
   • How did you show it?
   • What are some things we can do when we're feeling depressed?
     Mention that, while adults and some young people may withdraw during depression, many kids act angry when they are depressed in an attempt to deal with their feelings. They may even try antisocial things like shoplifting, getting drunk, or driving recklessly.

5. Ask volunteers to describe a happy time with their families.

6. Encourage participants to share any problems they're facing with either parent.
   • Are anyone's parents dating? What's that like?
   • Does anyone have a new stepmom or stepdad? Any problems there?
   • How about stepbrothers or stepsisters?

7. This afternoon we discussed acceptance. Ask the following questions:
   • How are you doing in accepting your parents' divorce?
   • Are there still some things that are hard to accept? How can we help?

8. We also discussed hope. Ask the following questions:
   • What hopes do you have for your own future (such as a fun vacation, college, dating, a happier family)?
   • Is it easy or hard for you to have hope right now? Why?

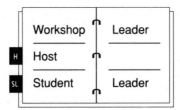

SAMPLE LETTER FROM STUDENT LEADERS TO PARTICIPANTS

Dear _____,

    I just wanted to drop you a quick note to thank you for coming to our group on (*Saturday*). You really helped with your (*smile, sense of humor, comments*). I hope you felt helped by the other kids who came to the workshop and by the teaching of the workshop leader.

                               Sincerely,

APPENDIX C
FRIDAY NIGHT/SATURDAY WORKSHOP

Perhaps you will find that a Friday night/Saturday workshop format fits best into your scheduling plans. If so, use the information and reproducible pages from the basic workshop to prepare for a Friday night/Saturday workshop: premise and goals, adolescent needs, time line, job descriptions, budget and publicity, physical arrangements, and refreshments.

Train the student leaders as you would for the basic workshop and provide the same handouts—except for the substitution of the Friday night/Saturday schedule, the alternate discussion questions, and the alternate follow-up letter, all found in Appendix C. Assign student leaders the same duties for greeting, discussion-leading, registering, and breaking the participants into small groups. For refreshments, assign a couple of student leaders to bring brownies for the break on Friday night and have a couple of others bring cut-up fruit for the Saturday morning break. In this format you will also have to make arrangements for lunch. Provide lunch, have students bring lunches from home, or order pizza!

Overview

The Friday night/Saturday workshop is divided into two separate days with one lecture session on Friday night and two on Saturday. The schedule is fleshed out and enhanced with mixers, group discussions, skits, an interview, and a panel discussion.

WL
H

Workshop   Leader

WL

Host

H

Student   Leader

OUTLINE OF
FRIDAY NIGHT/SATURDAY WORKSHOP

Friday

7:20   Adult and student leaders pray together.

7:30   Student leaders greet teen participants as they arrive, help them to register, and offer them refreshments.

8:00   Host welcomes group and leads *People Bingo* (pp. 88 and 122).

   Assigned student leaders divide participants into groups during the mixer (see p. 75, "Dividing Participants into Groups").

8:15   Workshop leader offers lectures and student leaders present skits on the first two stages of grief: denial and anger (lecture outline begins on p. 76).

9:00   Student leaders guide *Small-Group Discussion VI.*

9:40   Workshop leader conducts a discussion on *Dealing with Mom* (discussion outline on p. 77).

10:00   Ten-minute debriefing with student leaders.

Saturday

8:35   Adult and student leaders pray together.

8:45   Host leads *Slogan Game* (p. 89) and Good, *Clean Jokes* (p. 88).

9:00   Workshop leader offers lectures and student leaders present skits on next two stages of grief: bargaining and depression (lecture outline begins on p. 80).

9:45   Student leaders guide *Small-Group Discussion VII.*

10:30   Refreshment break.

10:45   Workshop leader conducts a discussion on *Dealing with Dad* (p. 80).

11:00   Workshop leader and student leaders organize *Family Sculpture* (p. 81)**.**

11:35   Ten-minute debriefing with student leaders.

11:45   Lunch break.

1:00   Host moderates an interview with a teen and parent (p. 90).

   Workshop leader hands out 3 x 5 cards and pencils for participants to write out questions for the upcoming panel.

1:30   Workshop leader offers lectures and student leaders present skits on the last two stages of grief: acceptance and hope (lecture outline begins on p. 83).

2:10   Workshop leader conducts discussion on *Keeping Out from Between Mom and Dad* (discussion outline on p. 83).

2:30   Student leaders guide *Small-Group Discussion VIII.*

3:10   Host moderates panel discussion (p. 90).

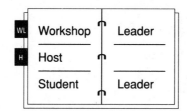

3:45   *Family Sculpture* (optional).

4:00   Workshop leader leads optional sharing time (p 77).

4:20   Participants fill in workshop evaluations (Appendix A).

4:30   Adjournment.

4:35   Final debriefing with student leaders (p. 78).

SL

Workshop	Leader
Host	
Student	Leader

STUDENT LEADERS' OUTLINE OF FRIDAY NIGHT/SATURDAY WORKSHOP

Friday

7:20   Adult and student leaders pray together.

7:30   Student leaders greet teen participants as they arrive, help them register, and offer them refreshments.

8:00   Host welcomes group and leads mixer.

      Assigned student leaders divide participants into groups during the mixer.

8:15   Workshop leader offers lectures and student leaders present skits on the first two stages of grief: denial and anger (skits on pp. 97–99).

9:00   Student leaders guide *Small-Group Discussion VI* (p. 135).

9:40   Workshop leader conducts a discussion on *Dealing with Mom*.

10:00   Ten-minute debriefing with student leaders.

Saturday

8:35   Adult and student leaders pray together.

8:45   Host leads mixers.

9:00   Workshop leader offers lectures and student leaders present skits on next two stages of grief: bargaining and depression (skits on pp. 100–103).

9:45   Student leaders guide *Small-Group Discussion VII* (p. 136).

10:30   Refreshment break.

10:45   Workshop leader leads a discussion on *Dealing with Dad*.

11:00   Workshop leader and student leaders organize *Family Sculpture*.

11:35   Ten-minute debriefing with student leaders.

11:45   Lunch break.

1:00   Host moderates an interview with a teen and parent.

      Workshop leader hands out 3 x 5 cards and pencils for participants to write out questions for the upcoming panel.

1:30   Workshop leader offers lectures and student leaders present skits on the last two stages of grief: acceptance and hope (skits on pp. 104–106).

2:10   Workshop leader conducts discussion on *Keeping Out from Between Mom and Dad*.

2:30   Student leaders guide *Small-Group Discussion VIII* (p. 137).

3:10   Host moderates panel discussion.

3:45   *Family Sculpture* (optional).

4:00   Workshop leader leads optional sharing time.

4:20   Participants fill in workshop evaluations.

4:30   Adjournment.

4:35   Final debriefing with student leaders.

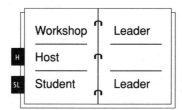

SMALL-GROUP DISCUSSION QUESTIONS VI

1. Begin by introducing yourself and telling a little about your own family and the reasons you volunteered to help with the workshop. Then explain these ground rules:
   - You don't have to talk if you don't want to.
   - Everything said here is confidential. None of it is to be repeated to *anyone* outside the group.
   - This is *our* group. We all share responsibility for its success.

2. When everyone is feeling comfortable, ask participants to
   - Tell where they live and go to school.
   - Describe their families and whom they live with.
   - Name things they like to do.
   - Tell how long ago their parents separated or divorced.
   - For volunteers only: Why do you think your parents split up?

3. Point out that tonight the group discussed denial and anger. Ask the following questions:
   - Did anything happen recently that you tried to pretend didn't happen? What was it?
   - Is anyone in your family denying the reality of your parents' divorce?
   - Did you get really angry recently? What was the problem?
   - How do you express anger?
   - What are some positive ways we can express anger in our families?

Workshop	Leader
H Host	
SL Student	Leader

SMALL-GROUP DISCUSSION QUESTIONS VII

1. Ask volunteers to share one idea they remember from last night's session.

2. Ask the group what changes they have seen in their parents during or since the divorce/separation. What changes have they seen in themselves?

3. Point out that this morning we talked about bargaining. Ask:
   • Has anyone tried to bargain for something recently with their parent or parents?
   • Did it have anything to do with the divorce?   What happened?

4. We also talked about how it's normal to feel depressed when your parents divorce. Ask the following questions:
   • Has anyone felt depressed recently?
   • How did you show it?
   • What are some things we can do when we're feeling depressed?
     Mention that, while adults and some young people may withdraw during depression, many kids act angry when they are depressed in an attempt to deal with their feelings. They may even try antisocial things like shoplifting, getting drunk, or driving recklessly.

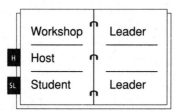

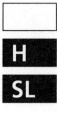

SMALL-GROUP DISCUSSION QUESTIONS VIII

1. Open the discussion by asking volunteers to describe a happy time with their families.

2. Encourage participants to share any problems they're facing with either parent.
   - Are anyone's parents dating? What's that like?
   - Does anyone have a new stepmom or stepdad? Any problems there?
   - How about stepbrothers or sisters?

3. Point out that this afternoon the workshop leader talked about parents "using" kids. Ask the following questions:
   - Has either of your parents ever tried to use you as a messenger, an informant, or a dumping ground for complaints?
   - How did it make you feel?
   - What are some ways we can get out from between our parents and their conflicts?

4. This afternoon we discussed acceptance. Ask the following questions:
   - How are you doing in accepting your parents' divorce?
   - Are there still some things that are hard to accept? How can we help?

5. We also discussed hope. Ask the following questions:
   - What hopes do you have for your own future (such as a fun vacation, college, dating, a happier family)?
   - Is it easy or hard for you to have hope right now? Why?

Workshop	Leader
H Host	
SL Student	Leader

SAMPLE LETTER FROM
STUDENT LEADERS TO PARTICIPANTS

Dear_____,

   I just wanted to drop you a quick note to thank you for coming to our group last weekend. You really helped with your (*smile, sense of humor, comments, etc.*). I hope you felt helped by the other kids who came to the workshop and by the teaching of the workshop leader.

                             Sincerely,

APPENDIX D
WEEKEND RETREAT WORKSHOP

Using a weekend retreat format for your workshop can allow you to get to know kids in a more intimate way. If you choose to run your workshop as a weekend retreat, you may still use the information and some of the reproducible pages from the basic workshop to prepare: premise and goals, adolescent needs, time line, job descriptions, budget and publicity, physical arrangements, and refreshments.

We have not attempted to give you detailed information on running retreats. The schedules do not reflect wake-up calls, breakfast times, or lights-out times. The schedules will, however, help you with the actual planning of the workshop. Suggestions for extra activities that you might like to add (special music and added games, for example) are purely optional; fill the time slots that are not directly related to the workshop with activities that suit your group.

Train the student leaders as you would for the basic workshop and provide the same handouts—except for the substitution of the weekend retreat schedule, the alternate discussion questions, and the alternate follow-up letter, all found in Appendix D. Assign student leaders the same duties for greeting, discussion-leading, registering, and breaking the participants into small groups. For refreshments, assign a couple of student leaders to bring cut-up fruit for the Saturday morning and Sunday morning refreshment breaks, or provide doughnuts and juice.

Overview

The weekend retreat workshop is held on a weekend and begins on Friday night and continues through lunch time on Sunday. The lectures are divided into four sessions (the fourth is on an added topic: forgiveness). There is room in the schedule for numerous activities which will include mixers and games, group discussions, skits, an interview, and a panel discussion, and may include much more.

WL	Workshop	Leader
H	Host	
	Student	Leader

OUTLINE OF
WEEKEND RETREAT WORKSHOP

Friday

6:50   Adult and student leaders pray together.

7:00   Assigned student leaders greet teen participants as they arrive and help them to register.

7:30   Host welcomes group and leads *People Bingo* (instructions on p. 88).
    Assigned student leaders divide participants into groups during the mixer (see p. 75, "Dividing Participants into Groups").

8:15   Workshop leader offers lectures and student leaders present skits on the first two stages of grief: denial and anger (lecture outline begins on p. 76).

9:00   Student leaders guide *Small-Group Discussion IX*.

9:40   Workshop leader conducts a discussion on *Dealing with Mom* (discussion outline on p. 77).

10:00   Ten-minute debriefing with student leaders.

Saturday

8:35   Adult and student leaders pray together.

8:45   Host leads *Slogan Game* (p. 89) and *Good, Clean Jokes* (p. 88).

9:00   Workshop leader offers lectures and student leaders present skits on next two stages of grief: bargaining and depression (lecture outline begins on p. 80).

9:45   Student leaders guide *Small-Group Discussion X*.

10:30   Refreshment break.

10:45   Workshop leader conducts a discussion on *Dealing with Dad* (p. 80).

11:00   Workshop leader and student leaders organize *Family Sculpture* (p. 81).

11:35   Ten-minute debriefing with student leaders.

11:45   Lunch break.

1:00   Host moderates an interview with a teen and parent (p. 90).

1:30   Free time.

5:00   Dinner.

6:00   Use for special music, singing, games.

7:00   Workshop leader offers lectures and student leaders present skits on the last two stages of grief: acceptance and hope (lecture outline begins on p. 83).

7:40   Workshop leader conducts discussion on *Keeping Out from Between Mom and Dad* (discussion outline on p. 83).

8:00   Student leaders guide *Small-Group Discussion XI*.

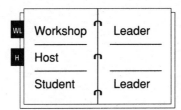

8:45   Optional *Family Sculpture*.

9:15   Workshop leader leads optional sharing time (p. 77).

9:35   Ten-minute debriefing with student leaders.

Sunday

8:35   Adult and student leaders pray together.

8:45   Host leads the game *Forgivers and Judgers* (p. 147), other games, or singing.

   Workshop leader hands out 3 x 5 cards and pencils for participants to write out questions for the upcoming panel.

9:15   Special music.

9:45   Host moderates panel discussion (p. 90).

10:30   Refreshment break.

10:45   Workshop leader guides participants through *TalkSheet*™ on forgiveness (pp. 148–151).

   Participants fill in workshop evaluations (Appendix A).

11:35   Final debriefing with student leaders.

11:45   Lunch and break camp.

Workshop | Leader

Host

SL | Student | Leader

STUDENT LEADERS' OUTLINE OF WEEKEND RETREAT WORKSHOP

Friday

6:50   Adult and student leaders pray together.

7:00   Student leaders greet teen participants as they arrive and help them register.

7:30   Host welcomes group and leads mixer.
        Assigned student leaders divide participants into groups during the mixer.

8:15   Workshop leader offers lectures and student leaders present skits on the first two stages of grief: denial and anger (skits on pp. 97–99).

9:00   Student Leaders guide *Small-Group Discussion IX* (p. 144).

9:40   Workshop leader conducts a discussion on *Dealing with Mom*.

10:00   Ten-minute debriefing with student leaders.

Saturday

8:35   Adult and student leaders pray together.

8:45   Host leads mixers.

9:00   Workshop leader offers lectures and student leaders present skits on next two stages of grief: bargaining and depression (skits on pp. 100–103).

9:45   Student leaders guide *Small-Group Discussion X* (p. 145).

10:30   Refreshment break.

10:45   Workshop leader conducts a discussion on *Dealing with Dad*.

11:00   Workshop leader and student leaders organize *Family Sculpture*.

11:35   Ten-minute debriefing with student leaders.

11:45   Lunch break.

1:00   Host moderates an interview with a teen and parent.

1:30   Free time.

5:00   Dinner break.

6:00   Use for special music, singing, games.

7:00   Workshop leader offers lectures and student leaders present skits on the last two stages of grief: acceptance and hope (skits on pp. 104–106).

7:40   Workshop leader conducts a discussion on *Keeping Out from Between Mom and Dad*.

8:00   Student leaders guide *Small-Group Discussion XI* (p. 146).

8:45   *Family Sculpture* (optional).

9:15   Workshop leader leads optional sharing time.

9:35   Ten-minute debriefing with student leaders.

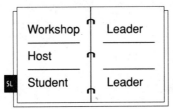

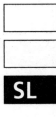

Sunday

8:35   Adult and student leaders pray together.

8:45   Host leads singing or games.

       Workshop leader hands out 3 x 5 cards and pencils for participants to write out questions for the upcoming panel.

9:15   Special music.

9:45   Host moderates panel discussion.

10:30   Refreshment break.

10:45   Workshop leader guides participants through *TalkSheet*™ on forgiveness.

       Participants fill in workshop evaluations.

11:35   Final debriefing with student leaders.

11:45   Lunch and break camp.

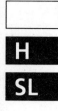

SMALL-GROUP DISCUSSION QUESTIONS IX

1. Begin by introducing yourself and telling a little about your own family and the reasons you volunteered to help with the workshop. Then explain these ground rules:
   - You don't have to talk if you don't want to.
   - Everything said here is confidential. None of it is to be repeated to *anyone* outside the group.
   - This is *our* group. We all share responsibility for its success.

2. When everyone is feeling comfortable, ask participants to
   - Tell where they live and go to school.
   - Describe their families and whom they live with.
   - Name things they like to do.
   - Tell how long ago their parents separated or divorced.
   - For volunteers only: Why do you think your parents split up?

3. Point out that tonight the group discussed denial and anger. Ask the following questions:
   - Did anything happen recently that you tried to pretend didn't happen? What was it?
   - Is anyone in your family denying the reality of your parents' divorce?
   - Did you get really angry recently? What was the problem?
   - How do you express anger?
   - What are some positive ways we can express anger in our families?

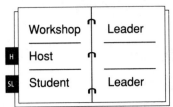

SMALL-GROUP DISCUSSION QUESTIONS X

1. Ask volunteers to share one idea they remember from any of the lectures so far.

2. Ask the group what changes they have seen in their parents during or since the divorce/separation. What changes have they seen in themselves?

3. Point out that this morning we talked about bargaining. Ask:
   - Has anyone tried to bargain for something recently with their parent or parents?
   - Did it have anything to do with the divorce? What happened?

4. We also talked about how it's normal to feel depressed when your parents divorce. Ask the following questions:
   - Has anyone felt depressed recently?
   - How did you show it?
   - What are some things we can do when we're feeling depressed?
   Mention that, while adults and some young people may withdraw during depression, many kids act angry when they are depressed in an attempt to deal with their feelings. They may even try antisocial things like shoplifting, getting drunk, or driving recklessly.

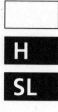

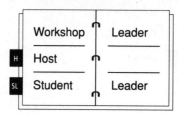

SMALL-GROUP DISCUSSION QUESTIONS XI

1. Open the discussion by asking volunteers to describe a happy time with their families.

2. Encourage participants to share any problems they're facing with either parent.
   - Are anyone's parents dating? What's that like?
   - Does anyone have a new stepmom or stepdad? Any problems there?
   - How about stepbrothers or stepsisters?

3. Point out that tonight the workshop leader talked about parents using kids. Ask the following questions:
   - Has either of your parents ever tried to use you as a messenger, an informant, or a dumping ground for complaints?
   - How did it make you feel?
   - What are some ways we can get out from between our parents and their conflicts?

4. Tonight we discussed acceptance. Ask the following questions:
   - How are you doing in accepting your parents' divorce?
   - Are there still some things that are hard to accept? How can we help?

5. We also discussed hope. Ask the following questions:
   - What hopes do you have for your own future (such as a fun vacation, college, dating, a happier family)?
   - Is it easy or hard for you to have hope right now? Why?

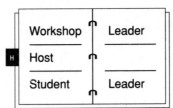

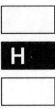

FORGIVERS AND JUDGERS

To reinforce the values of affirmation and forgiveness, divide your group into two or more teams. Set up some kind of target or dart board for each team (foam targets and balls with velcro strips would be best). Then have a contest to see which team can score the most points.

But before the contest begins, give each kid a slip of paper with an assignment as either a *forgiver* or a *judger*. When players on their own team don't make a perfect hit, the *forgivers* are supposed to say things like, "That's okay," "Keep trying your best," and "We still like you." *Judgers* are supposed to say things like, "Can't you do better than that?" "That was a bad throw. We'll never win," and "Whose team are you on, anyway?"

After the game is over and the scores are added up, ask the group these questions:

1. On a scale of one to ten, how much did you enjoy this game? Why?

2. What difference did the *forgivers* make? Why?

3. What difference did the *judgers* make? Why?

4. Did you enjoy being a *forgiver?* A *judger?*

WL Workshop ⌐ Leader

Host ⌐

Student ⌐ Leader

HOW TO USE A TALKSHEET™

A TalkSheet™ is a ready-to-use discussion starter. Make a copy of the TalkSheet™ for each participant. Try the TalkSheet™ yourself first. Fill it out as if you were one of the kids in your group. This role playing will give you firsthand knowledge of what you will ask the kids to do. As you fill out the TalkSheet, you may think of additional questions, activities, or applicable Scriptures.

Give the participants time to work on their TalkSheets™ individually or in small groups. Or lead the whole group to answer one question at a time. Whatever your plan, be sure to allow enough time for the kids to thoughtfully answer each question in writing *before* the discussion.

A TalkSheet™ is not a quiz. Let your kids know that you are asking for opinions. Explain that not only are all opinions worthwhile, but that the students are responsible to contribute their opinions to the rest of the group. Hearing the reactions of other kids is part of their healing process.

Here are some additional tips on leading effective discussions.

- *Divide large groups.* If your group is larger than fifteen or twenty kids, you may want to divide into the discussion groups you've used throughout the weekend and prepare the student leaders to lead the discussion.

- *Keep the group on the topic.* Gently redirect the discussion if the group wanders from the topic.

- *Affirm everyone who contributes.* Even if you don't agree with some of the comments and ideas the kids share, let them know that you appreciate their thoughtful openness. It's better to remain neutral than to shut off the flow of dialogue by judging an opinion as right or wrong. Just thank kids for sharing, and do it sincerely.

- *Don't set yourself up as an authority.* Be a co-learner and facilitator. Give input when it's appropriate, but save outright teaching until an appropriate time.

- *Actively listen to each person.* Look the kids in the eyes when they talk. Rephrase their comments sometimes just to show that you really are listening.

- *Don't force anyone to talk.* Everyone has the right to pass. You can nudge the group by asking certain kids for their opinions, but if they are reluctant, don't push them.

- *Don't allow one person to monopolize the discussion.* Most groups have a motor-mouth who likes to talk. Direct questions to some of the others and encourage everyone to participate.

- *Allow humor when appropriate.* A good laugh loosens up a tense discussion.

- *Don't be afraid of silence.* If no one has anything to say right away, just wait. Sometimes rephrasing the question starts the flow of talk, but don't be intimidated by silence. You may even want to discuss the silence itself.

The above information about TalkSheets™ as well as the leader aids are adapted from *Up Close & Personal: How to Build Community in Your Youth Group* by Wayne Rice, copyright 1989 by Youth Specialties, Inc., published by Zondervan Publishing House, 1415 Lake Drive, S.E., Grand Rapids, Michigan 49506. Used by permission.

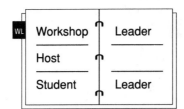

FORGIVENESS TALKSHEET™
LEADER'S GUIDE

The following TalkSheet™ focuses on forgiveness, raising questions that help participants think through their ideas before sharing them with the group. The numbered notes correspond to questions on the kids' TalkSheets.™ Use them to stimulate your thoughts as you prepare to guide the discussion.

Question #1: God forgives us because he loves us and because Jesus paid for our sins on the cross. Other statements are true statements (God wants us to love him, for instance), but they are not the reasons why he forgives us. Emphasize to the kids that sin *is* a big deal and that sins are *not* easy for God to forgive. They cost the suffering and death of God's son, Jesus Christ. But because of the price that was paid, God is "faithful and just and will forgive us our sins" (I John 1:9).

Question #2: Have the kids share their answers. The main idea is that *Christians should forgive in response to and in the same spirit as God's forgiveness.*

Question #3: Ask two of the student leaders to role-play this parable. Cast one of them as the king and another as the servant who owed 10,000 talents. The scene starts with verse 32, when the king calls the servant in. The servant must convince the king that what he did (not forgiving the fellow servant's small debt) was right.

Jesus taught that we are obligated to forgive each other in light of the forgiveness that God has given to us. Have the kids share their answers to the questions and their interpretations of the parable's moral. Record them on the chalkboard so that everyone can see them during the remainder of the discussion.

Question #4: Talk briefly about why some chose forgiving (or asking forgiveness) as the more difficult. The point is that both require effort.

Question #5: There is a difference between peacemakers and peace-lovers. Most think of themselves as peace-lovers, but it is only the peacemakers who are blessed, says Jesus. Forgiving qualifies you as a peacemaker and results in blessing from God.

The flip-side is that if we don't forgive, we receive the opposite of blessing—unhappiness, bitterness, resentment, hatred, and anger. The choice is ours.

Question #6: Once the kids have written down the hurts they have received and the hurts they have given to others, read Ephesians 4:31,32 aloud to them. Remind them that God has asked us to forgive because it is in our best interest to do so. Only when we forgive are we released to move on in our lives, freed from the emotional bondage we are under when we hold on to anger, bitter resentment, or hurt.

Now ask the kids to wad up the card that lists their worst hurts and the names of those who have hurt them. Tell them the physical act of getting rid of the cards helps them to emotionally let go of the hurts. Pass a big coffee can around the room for everyone to toss their wadded up cards into. Ask for everyone to pray silently, telling God that they want to be set free from their anger and sadness over those hurts, and that they forgive the people who have hurt them in those ways. Light a match and toss it into the can. (If you're outside you can follow the burning

by scattering the ashes into the wind.)

Return the kids' attention to their second card—the one listing three hurts they have given someone. Ask them to think through what they need to do both to restore their relationships with those people and to be part of healing those people they've hurt. Tell them to make notes to help themselves remember what the Lord is urging them to do. Ask them to either put the cards in their Bibles, purses, or wallets—any place that they'll come across them often once they get back home. Let them know that any of the staff will be glad to help them think of ideas for restoring a relationship if they're stuck.

FORGIVENESS

1 **Read 1 John 1:9.** Why do you think God is willing to forgive us for our sins? Choose the best answer or answers below.
☐ Sin is no big deal to God.
☐ Sins are easy for God to forgive.
☐ God wants us to love him.
☐ God loves us.
☐ God wants to give us a second chance.
☐ God knows what it's like to be a human being.
☐ God wants us to be indebted to him.
☐ Jesus paid for our sins on the cross.
☐ God promised to forgive sins, and he won't break a promise.

2 **Read Colossians 3:12–14.** According to these verses, why should Christians forgive each other?

3 **Use Matthew 18:21–35 to answer the following questions:**
What was Jesus teaching in verse 22 when he answered "not seven, but seventy-seven times?"
a. Keep forgiving until the 78th time.
b. There should be no limit to forgiveness.
c. Don't ask stupid questions.

In the parable that Jesus told, who is the worst person?
a. The king (the master).
b. The servant who owed 10,000 talents.
c. The fellow servant who owed 100 denarii.
d. The other servants who blew the whistle on the first servant.

Rewrite the moral of the story (verse 35) in your own words. _____
_____
_____

4 Which is most difficult for you:
☐ To forgive someone?
☐ To ask for their forgiveness?

5 Read Matthew 5:9. Now check the statement that best applies to you.
☐ I always do whatever I can to make peace with others.
☐ I sometimes try to make peace with others.
☐ I rarely try to make peace with others.
☐ I never try to make peace with others.

6 **Read Ephesians 4:31–32.** Is there a person you need to forgive? A person you need to ask for forgiveness? On your three-by-five card, write down three of your worst hurts that you want to begin to be healed from. Beside the hurt write the names of the people who hurt you—those people whom you must forgive in order to make peace and make way for healing.

On your second card write out three of the worst ways you've hurt someone. Beside each of the hurts write the initials of the person you hurt in that way.

The above information about TalkSheets as well as the leader aids are adapted from *Up Close & Personal: How to Build Community in Your Youth Group* by Wayne Rice, copyright 1989 by Youth Specialties, Inc., published by Zondervan Publishing House, 1415 Lake Drive, S.E., Grand Rapids, Michigan 49506. Used by permission.

APPENDIX E
BIBLIOGRAPHY

BIBLIOGRAPHY

Arnold, William V. *When Your Parents Divorce*. Louisville, Ky.: Christian Care Books, Westminster/John Knox Press, 1980.

Brogan, John P. and Ula Marden. *Kids Guide to Divorce*. New York: Crest, Fawcett/Ballantine, 1986.

Dycus, Jim and Barbara Dycus. *Children of Divorce*. Elgin, Ill.: David C. Cook, 1987.

Egan, Gerard. *The Skilled Helper: Model Skills and Methods for Effective Helping*. Pacific Grove, Calif.: Brooks-Cole/Wadsworth, 1985.

Francke, Linda Bird. *Growing Up Divorced*. New York: Crest, Fawcett/Ballantine, 1984.

Frydenger, Tom and Adrienne Frydenger. *The Blended Family*. Old Tappan, N.J.: Chosen Books/Revell, 1985.

Gardner, Richard A., *The Boys and Girls Book about Divorce*. New York: Bantam/Doubleday/Dell, 1971.

——— . *The Boys and Girls Book about One-Parent Families*. 1978 reprint. Cresskill, N.J.: Creative Therapeutics, 1983.

——— . *The Parents Book about Divorce*. New York: Bantam/Doubleday/Dell, 1982.

Hart, Archibald. *Children and Divorce*. Waco, Tex.: Word, 1985.

Kalter, Neil. *Growing Up with Divorce*. New York: Free Press/Macmillan, 1989.

Krementz, Jill. *How It Feels When Parents Divorce*. New York: Knopf/Random House, 1984.

Kubler-Ross, Elizabeth. *On Death and Dying*. New York: Macmillan, 1970.

Nouwen, Henri. *The Wounded Healer: Ministry in Contemporary Society*. New York: Bantam/Doubleday/Dell, 1979.

Phillips, Carolyn E. *Our Family Got a Divorce*. Ventura, Calif.: Regal/Gospel Light, 1979.

Ricci, Isolina. *Mom's House, Dad's House: Making Shared Custody Work*. New York: Macmillan, 1980.

Smoke, Jim. *Growing Through Divorce*. New York: Bantam/Doubleday/Dell, 1986.

Tickfer, Mildred. *Healing the Hurt: For Teenagers Whose Parents Are Divorced*. Grand Rapids: Baker, 1985.

Vigeveno, H. S. and Anne Claire. *No One Gets Divorced Alone*. Ventura, Calif.: Regal/Gospel Light, 1987.

Wallerstein, Judith S. and Sandra Blakeslee. *Second Chances: Men, Women, & Children a Decade after Divorce*. New York: Ticknor & Fields/Houghton Mifflin Co., 1989.

Wallerstein, Judith S. and Joan Berlin Kelly. *Surviving the Breakup: How Children and Parents Cope with Divorce*. Hobart, Ind.: Basic Books, Inc., 1982.